SEARCH FOR THE SEVEN CITIES

SEARCH FOR THE SEVEN CITIES

The Opening of the American Southwest

JOHN UPTON TERRELL

With drawings by
W. K. Plummer

HARCOURT BRACE JOVANOVICH, INC.

NEW YORK

CRB

Curriculum-Related Books are relevant
to current interests of young people
and to topics in the school curriculum.

Maps by Graphic 70

First Edition

Library of Congress Catalog Card Number: 78–128367

Printed in the United States of America

ISBN 0–15–271210–0

CONTENTS

LIST OF MAPS

SEARCH FOR THE SEVEN CITIES

1 / A BOYHOOD MEMORY

Tejo was an Indian slave owned by a Spaniard, Nuño Beltrán de Guzmán, and he told a tale destined to set off a chain of dramatic, tragic, and historically important events in New Spain.

Guzmán was an influential politician notorious for his illegal and barbarous conquests. In 1527 he was Governor of the Mexican Province of Pánuco and President of the *Audencia,* the board that directed the affairs of the colony. The positions gave him supreme powers in Pánuco, and he wielded them with wanton disregard for either the State or the people under his rule. He considered himself a god to whom all must pay tribute and obeisance. In a foul mood one day, Guzmán hanged several natives who did not sweep the street before him as he passed through their village. He sold and bartered thousands of Indian men, women and children into slavery throughout the West Indies for his personal gain. In time his cruel treatment of the Indians caused high officers of the Church to register a strong protest with the Spanish King, and Guzmán was ordered to govern his territory with justice and in accordance with colonial laws.

The reprimand, however, had little effect on him. If he was obliged to curb his brutal practices somewhat in Pánuco, he was not prevented from looking farther afield for opportunities to gratify his avarice. Guzmán revealed that he was thinking of taking a treasure hunting and slaving expedition into regions of western New Spain (Mexico) of which little, if anything, was known.

Here Tejo came upon the stage of recorded history. When he heard of Guzmán's plans, he asked for permission to tell him a story, most probably with the hope of gaining some favor for himself. The request was granted, and Tejo found Guzmán a most attentive listener.

He was, said Tejo, the son of a trader who had been dead a number of years. Often when he was a boy, his father had taken him along on trading trips into the wilderness. One journey had been longer than all the others. On it they had traveled for more than forty days to the north, passing through a desolate land, a desert, in which nothing grew but a few very small plants. At last they had reached a bountiful country with many people who lived in large towns that were comparable in size to the city of Mexico. They had taken with them packs of the beautiful feathers and plumes of tropical birds, and in exchange for these they had obtained turquoises and stones even more precious, as well as articles of gold and silver. Tejo said that he could remember seeing streets of

Guzmán listened eagerly as Tejo told of seven large cities in a rich land north of New Spain.

silver workers, and that in this rich country the large cities were *seven in number.*

Seven Cities! Guzmán's cold blood grew hot from excitement, when he heard magic words. Like every other conquistador, he knew well the legend of the Seven Cities of Antilia, which for so many generations had inspired all adventurers and filled them with dreams.

According to the legend, in the eighth century, after the Moors had invaded Spain and Portugal, oppressed Christians led by the Archbishop of Oporto and six other bishops had sailed westward into the unknown Ocean Sea and had discovered the luxurious island of Antilia. Each of the seven bishops founded and ruled a city, and the whole Island of the Seven Cities became a Utopian commonwealth, fabulously rich in gold and jewels and supplied with all manner of food and comforts.

Although it had been shown on numerous maps, the Island of Antilia had never been found. The name Antilles had been given to the West Indian Islands, but that had been a mistake. Neither Columbus nor any of the explorers who had followed him had discovered evidence showing that Portuguese once had inhabited the islands.

Now Guzmán reasoned that with all the darkness that remained in the New World, with all the countries that remained to be opened, who was to say that the Seven Cities would not some day be found? Indeed, who was to say that an ignorant Indian slave had not seen them? Guzmán knew what he would do, and he wasted no time getting started.

Late in 1529, he set out from central Mexico with four hundred Spanish soldiers, and several thousand Indian servants, burden bearers, and livestock tenders, harboring a burning hope of being the discoverer and the conqueror of the legendary cities. Tejo was taken along as a guide, but it soon became apparent that although he might have traveled through the wilderness as a boy with his father, he had forgotten most of what he had learned of the trails. He knew, however, the general direction to be taken. It was necessary to cross Mexico to the South Sea [Gulf of California], and then turn north. Guzmán did not argue.

Perhaps Tejo had gone with his father to trade with the Pueblo Indians in country that one day would comprise the immense States of Arizona and New Mexico. If he had not, it was obvious that he knew of them and their culture and that they lived in large permanent towns. The truth was, of course—although Guzmán would never know it—that this was common knowledge among the Indians of northern Mexico, for trade between them and the Pueblos had been carried on for countless centuries before the time of Columbus. Whatever the case, if Tejo had not seen the Seven Cities with his own eyes, he was far from being an ignorant Indian. Indeed he was clever, for he knew what Guzmán wanted to hear.

As he pushed westward through some of the highest ranges and the roughest terrain in Mexico, Guzmán acted in character. He gave vent to incredible barbarities, destroying Indian settlements, burning fields, and inflicting unspeakable cruelties on all natives encountered. Somewhere along this trail of waste, bloodshed, and terrible suffering, the unfortunate, and probably terrorized, Tejo died.

Guzmán plunged on, unjustifiably concluding from Tejo's imprecise statements that once he had come in sight of the sea he would find an easy passage northward to his goal. He would quickly learn that the opposite was true.

Pedro de Castañeda, who lived in Mexico at the time, wrote that after Guzmán and his strong force broke through to the Pacific and reached Culiacán they tried to go on. But they "found the difficulties very great, because the mountain chains which are near that sea are so rough that it was impossible, after great labor, to find a passageway in that region. His whole army had to stay in the district of Culiacán for so long on this account that some rich men who were with him . . . changed their minds, and every day became more anxious to return."

While facing this disappointing situation, Guzmán received bad news from Mexico City. His greatest political enemy, Hernando Cortez, the conqueror of Mexico, recently had returned from Spain with a new high title bestowed on him by the King. Cortez also had been granted powers which put him in a position to retaliate for the many injuries Guzmán had inflicted upon him.

Guzmán, fearing that Cortez "would want to pay him back in the same way, or worse," decided that it would be wise for him to remain in the remote west—at least for the time being. He abandoned his attempt to reach the Seven Cities, but he continued his trade in human beings, sending parties of slave hunters far north into territories now in the State of Sonora, which were inhabited by Piman Indians. Several settlements he founded would become important Mexican cities. He established his own headquarters at Compostela.

When Guzmán was ordered by the colonial court to return to Mexico City, he refused to obey. Eventually he was arrested, stripped of his rank and authority, and confined to prison. He died in exile, penniless, friendless and despised.

But the dream of finding the Seven Cities did not die. Indeed, even before the avaricious Guzmán had been forcibly driven from office, events had transpired which, once more, caused the legend to dominate the mind of every conquistador and adventurer in Mexico.

2 / UNLOCKING THE GATE

Near the end of the year 1535 four strange men, followed by a throng of Indians, came out of western Texas into the valley of the Río Grande. Three of them had scraggly beards. Long hair brushed their shoulders and was held by thongs of deer hide. Except for skin breechcloths, they were naked. Their bodies were lean, hard, lithe, and deeply burned by years of exposure. From their necks crudely made wooden crosses were suspended on cords of woven animal hair. They were Spaniards—Álvar Nuñez Cabeza de Vaca, Andrés Dorantes de Carranca and Alonzo del Castillo Maldonado.

The fourth man was even more startling to behold. He was the color of ebony, and he had a large head of intensely black hair adorned with bright feathers. His powerful muscles rippled, his white teeth gleamed, and he strode in a regal manner. He was a native of Morocco, the slave of Dorantes, called simply Estevanico the Black.

They were the first men of the Old World to cross the continent north of Mexico, and the first to reach the perimeter of the land that one day would be the Southwest of the United States.

More than seven years earlier—in the spring of 1528—the expedition of Pánfilo de Narváez had landed near Tampa Bay, Florida, and within a few days had set out northward through the unknown American wilderness in search of treasure. The four men on the Río Grande in December, 1535, were the only survivors of the three hundred soldiers and adventurers who had started on the conquest.

In northern Florida a number of the expedition members had been killed in fights with Indians and others had died of malnutrition, dysentery, and fever. Desperately attempting to save themselves, the remaining men had constructed crude boats and had made their way westward in them, along the coast of the Gulf of Mexico, hoping to reach a Mexican settlement. The boats had been destroyed in a November storm on the swampy coast of Texas.

Not until September, 1534, six years after the disaster, were Cabeza de Vaca, Dorantes, Castillo and Estevanico —the only men of the company still alive—able to escape from the Texas coastal tribes and start on the journey that would bring them fame.

More than a year later they came to the Río Grande near the mouth of the Conchos River, which empties into it from Mexico. Turning upstream they had found people who lived in permanent towns built of adobe and

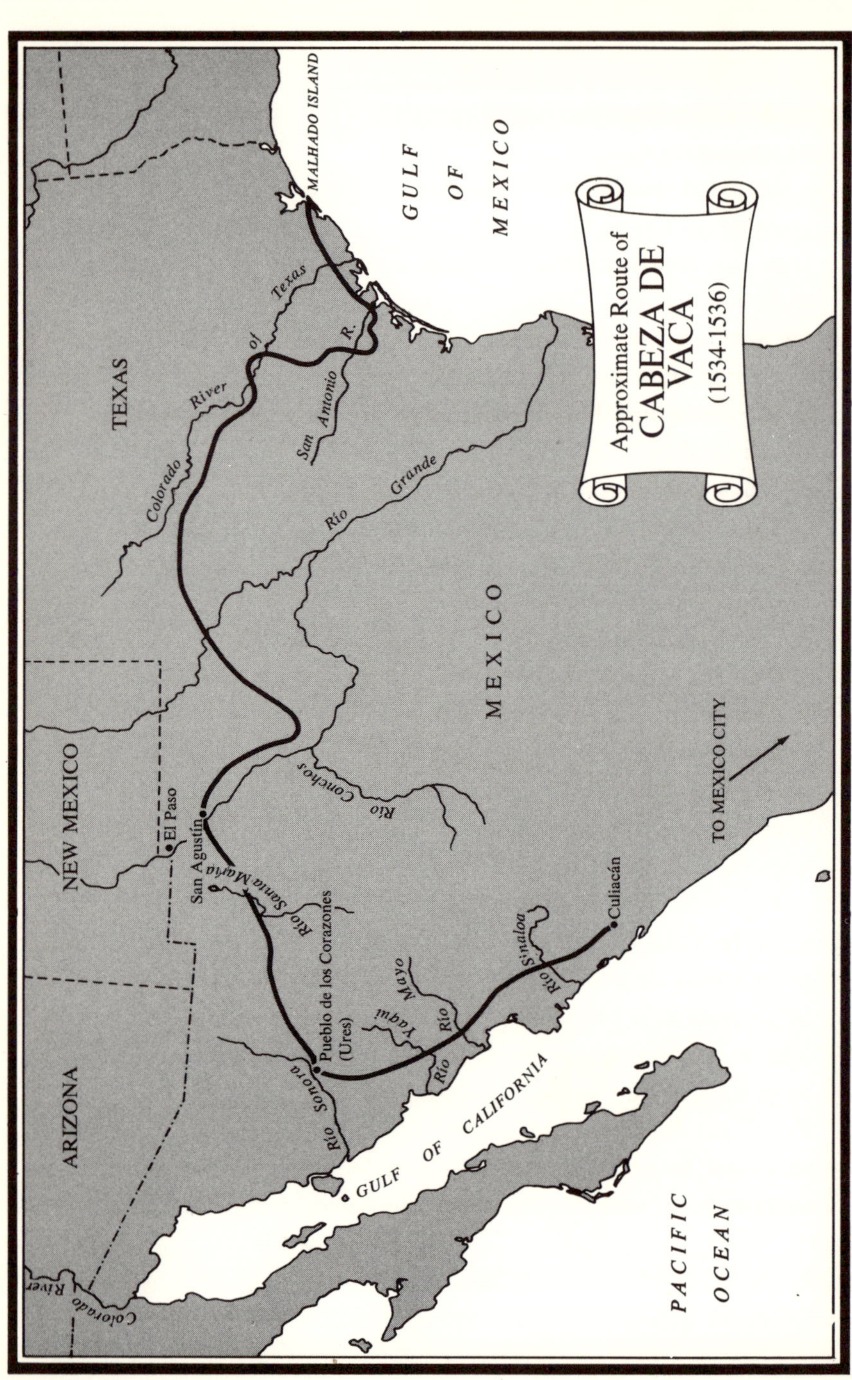

Approximate Route of
CABEZA DE VACA
(1534-1536)
MALHADO ISLAND
GULF OF MEXICO
TEXAS
River of Texas
Colorado River
San Antonio R.
Rio Grande
NEW MEXICO
El Paso
San Agustín
Rio Conchos
MEXICO
Rio Santa María
Pueblo de los Corazones
(Ures)
Rio Sonora
Rio Yaqui
Rio Mayo
Rio Sinaloa
Culiacán
TO MEXICO CITY
ARIZONA
Colorado River
GULF OF CALIFORNIA
PACIFIC OCEAN

rock. They had discovered the Jumanos, Pueblo Indians of the Southwest.

In his *Relación,* an invaluable account of their incomparable journey, Cabeza de Vaca gave the first description of southwestern Indians ever printed. The Jumanos, he wrote, "have the finest persons of any people we saw, of the greatest activity and strength, who best understood us and intelligently answered our inquiries." After learning that each spring the Jumanos traveled northward to the Great Plains to hunt buffalo, Cabeza de Vaca gave them the name of the Cow Nation.

Like other tribes they encountered in Texas, the Jumanos thought the four strangers had come out of the sky and were powerful medicine men. In any town they entered, they found the Jumanos waiting indoors for them. In each house men, women and children were seated on the floor facing a wall, their heads down. Their possessions had been gathered and placed in the center of the room. In this way way everything they owned was presented to the visitors, who, after accepting the gifts with signs of gratefulness, returned them.

For two summers no rain had fallen in the Río Grande Valley, and the Jumanos had not been able to grow maize or other crops. Yet, they had grain stored in large pots and baskets. When Cabeza de Vaca inquired where it came from, he was told that it had been obtained in trade from other Indians living farther up the Río Grande in a land where there had been sufficient moisture to grow corn. If the Sun Men would continue up the river, said the Jumanos, they would reach a country well populated, find even larger towns in which they would be well received and given valuable things, such as cotton mantles, buffalo robes and bright stones. They had been told of the great pueblos of the upper Río Grande which would figure so importantly in the history of the next few years.

For nearly three weeks the four Sun Men traveled up the valley of the Río Grande. Then they reached the place where they were obliged to make a vital decision. At the time they were probably only a few miles below El Paso del Norte, on the trail that later would become a part of the main Spanish road from Mexico City to Santa Fe.

The Jumanos told them that going on north they would encounter colder weather and snow. Blizzards already might have occurred. Westward was only a forbidding land in which there was little water and few people. It was an endless desert, and the Jumanos counseled them against entering it. They were urged to remain where they were until spring when it would be possible to travel safely in any direction they desired.

Cabeza de Vaca had no intention of passing another winter in idleness. He weighed the information thoughtfully. The Río Grande ran far to the north, but the Jumanos knew of no sea in that direction. The only sea of which they had heard, but had never seen, was an incalculable distance to the west. Their only hope of salvation lay in reaching the Pacific, for they knew that Spanish ports had been established on the western coast of Mexico. Going farther north would be a circuitous route to their goal, even though in that direction they could be assured of food and protection. They would go directly westward.

It was a bold and dangerous decision, but once the Spaniards had agreed on it they did not hesitate. They left the Río Grande near a village known today as San Augustín, about twenty miles south of Ciudad Juárez. With Jumanos guiding them, they followed a faint trail toward the southwest, across the vast desert reaches of the present Mexican State of Chihuahua. Desert trails change only when the waterholes along them change. The trail they took from San Augustín is still there, still followed. It took them to the green oasis of Samala-yuca.

For seventeen days they pressed steadily on, passing through soft, blowing white sand hills, and passing the salt lake of the Salado, where there were a few sweet water pools. Thirsty, dirty, burned by blowing sand, and bone-weary, they reached the Santa María, a trickle called a river that flowed two hundred miles to its death in the desert. They came to a land which had been eaten by fire—a fantastic land of great red and golden cones, holed rocks, pumice walls, cinder hills. Mesas were the color of dried blood. They trudged through saffron, topaz and slate scars, over rusted ridges. Distant benches were bathed in violet mists, and the valley floors were covered with olive blankets of sage and yellow cacti and gray-green cedars. There were days without water, when alkali whitened their faces and seared their eyes and mouths, days when the sun ran in red fire over the buttes. Always overhead the buzzards circled on motionless wings waiting for them to drop.

Seventeen days to the Santa María, and then seventeen more they went on westward, until one day as the sun went down they saw ahead the peaks of a great mountain range. They had come in sight of the towering Sierra Madre.

In the eastern reaches of the mountains, said Cabeza de Vaca, they "found a people who for the third part of a year eat nothing but the powder of straw, and, that being the season we passed, we also had to eat of it." Farther on in the mountains, however, the country grew greener. They found running streams, they saw birds and game animals, and they passed through forests and across high meadowlands. They had crossed the divide and were on the Pacific slope. At last they traveled down a long valley, and once more they came upon people dwelling in permanent villages, where there were storage bins filled with maize.

These people were the Opata, who spoke a dialect of the Piman language. "They gave us," said Cabeza de Vaca, "a large quantity in grain and flour, pumpkins, beans, and shawls of cotton. With all these we loaded our [Jumano] guides, who went back the happiest creatures on earth. We gave thanks to God, our Lord, for having brought us where we had found so much food."

They were in the valley of the Yaqui, a river flowing toward the setting sun and the South Sea, the Pacific. It was late in January, 1536, when their Pima guides brought them to a pueblo near the present town of Ures on the Río Sonora. En route they had "continually found settled domiciles, with plenty of maize and beans. The people gave us many deer and cotton shawls better than those of New Spain, many beads and certain corals found on the South Sea, and fine turquoises that come from the north."

In the pueblo near Ures two significant incidents occurred. Among the gifts which the generous people bestowed upon Cabeza de Vaca were five bright green stones, shaped like arrowheads, that were used in religious rituals. He wrote that they "seemed to be precious," and might be emeralds.* He asked "whence they got these; and they said the stones were brought from some lofty mountains that stand toward the north, where were populous towns and very large houses, and they were purchased with plumes and the feathers of parrots." He had been told of the pueblos of Arizona and New Mexico which contained buildings four and five stories in height, and now it appeared that precious stones were to be found in them.

The other important incident that took place at the Ures pueblo was an extraordinary feast, at which six hundred roasted deer hearts were prepared for the main course. Cabeza de Vaca, therefore, called the place *Pueblo de los Corazones,* City of the Hearts, and in subsequent years it would be the scene of dramatic events.

As they went on south they came upon indisputable

* They were probably malachites, a green basic carbonate of copper ore used for making ornaments.

evidence that Guzmán's slave hunters had been in the country. Cabeza de Vaca wrote:

> "We passed through many territories, and found them all vacant; their inhabitants wandered fleeing among the mountains, without daring to have houses or till the earth for fear of Christians.
>
> "The sight was one of infinite pain to us, a land very fertile and beautiful, abounding in springs and streams, the hamlets deserted and burned, the people thin and weak, all fleeing or in concealment.
>
> "As they did not plant, they appeased their keen hunger by eating roots and the bark of trees . . . They brought shawls of those they had concealed because of the Christians, presenting them to us, and they related how the Christians at other times had come through the land, destroying and burning the towns, carrying away half the men, and all the women and the boys . . . We found them so alarmed they dared not remain anywhere."

They did not fear Cabeza de Vaca and his companions, however, for word had gone ahead that they were kindly and peaceful men and were vigorously opposed to the slave trade. Several hundred Indians traveled with them, feeling secure in their presence. Cabeza de Vaca was filled with indignation and sorrow at knowledge of the cruelty of his countrymen, and he was moved to write: "Thence it may at once be seen that, to bring all these people to be Christians and to the obedience of the Imperial Majesty, they must be won by kindness, which is a way certain, and no other is."

Few conquistadors would heed these words. But he both spoke and wrote other words to which all Spaniards in Mexico were thoughtfully and excitedly attentive. "Throughout this region," Cabeza de Vaca said, "wheresoever the mountains extend, we saw clear traces of gold and lead, iron, copper and other metals. The people of the fixed residences regard silver and gold with indifference, nor can they conceive of any use for them."

On a day near the middle of March, 1536, somewhere along the Río Sinaloa, twenty Spanish horsemen were startled to see a gaunt bearded white man and an immense black Moor dressed in animal skins appear without warning out of a thicket. Behind them came a group of Indians.

Cabeza de Vaca told of the meeting in this way: "They stood staring at me a length of time, so confounded that they neither hailed me nor drew near to make an inquiry." There were tears in his eyes, and his voice faltered, as he spoke to them in Spanish.

As they went on through Culiacán, Compostela, Guadalajara and Morelia, along the road known as the Camino Real, thousands of people—Indians, Spaniards, and their bemuddled offspring—lined the streets and the roads of the countryside to catch a glimpse of the celebrated wanderers.

They reached Mexico City on July 24, 1536, and were borne along the avenues with cheers and waving flags. They were, said Cabeza de Vaca, "very handsomely treated" by the Viceroy, Don Antonio Mendoza, and the next day a great celebration with a jousting of bulls was held in their honor.

On the Río Sinaloa, Cabeza de Vaca and Estevanico
suddenly came upon a group of Spanish soldiers.

3 / THE CAUTIOUS VICEROY

Mexico City in the summer of 1536 was wild with excitement. Reports that Cabeza de Vaca and his companions had actually seen the Seven Cities spread like fire driven by high wind through prairie grass. It was said that if they had possessed any means of transporting it they would have brought with them an inconceivably immense fortune. Young noblemen and common adventurers alike claimed that they had heard the four men tell of fording streams that flowed in beds of solid gold, of seeing Indian children playing with diamonds, pearls and emeralds which had been thrown away as worthless, of having passed hills of silver and at least one mountain which contained so many jewels of all kinds that one dared not look at it in sunlight for fear of being blinded.

According to these windbags, the Viceroy was planning to send a great expedition to the north to harvest the incomparable treasures and to conquer the rich lands, all to the glory of King and Country. The Viceroy, of course, would reserve modest fortunes for himself and the lucky men permitted to participate in the conquest. Another Peru, another Mexico, another West Indies, another Ecuador, had been found. Hail to Cabeza de Vaca! Hail to the Viceroy! Drink to the greatness of Spain!

The Viceroy Mendoza, pacing the polished floors of his grand palace, burdened with the responsibilities of his high office, at the time had no such plans, even if the thoughts had crossed his mind. He had been in Mexico only a year, and he was still uneasy in the face of the many complex and difficult problems confronting him. It was very pleasant to think about taking possession of new lands and acquiring treasures for the Crown—it was, after all, his duty to increase as well as preserve the Royal estate. But he had no intention of plunging into an expensive conquest without adequate preparations and, even more important, without any assurance that he had a reasonable chance of succeeding in the undertaking.

Mendoza could safely assume, and presumably he did, that he had not been made the first Viceroy of New Spain, and the most powerful man in the New World, only because he was a nobleman whose loyalty to the Sovereign was unquestionable. He had also been chosen because of his integrity, political astuteness and competence as an administrator, and he did not propose to destroy the trust and faith which the King held in him.

There was no basis whatsoever for the rumors and gossip that had turned Mexico City into a feverish capital.

Neither Cabeza de Vaca, nor any of his three companions, had told fabulous tales of the country through which they had passed on their long journey. Every statement they had made had been conservative and qualified with the reminder that any information they had received from Indians had been given to them by signs, and they could not vouch for its accuracy.

None of the four men had claimed to have factual knowledge of large cities, or that they had seen streets of silver workers, or encountered people who ate from golden dishes and possessed priceless jewels. The most they had said was that they had seen some indications that the northern countries might contain valuable resources. They had seen people who lived in permanent houses in extremely fertile valleys, who had maize and other wholesome foodstuffs. They had seen turquoises and cotton blankets of excellent quality. They had been told that farther north than they had traveled were large and prosperous towns, with buildings four and five stories high, but they had not seen them. They had seen what they believed to be clear traces of valuable metals, but the only evidence of mineral resources they themselves had acquired had been some scoria of iron, some small bags of mica, some galena with which the natives painted their bodies, some turquoises, and five green arrowheads which might have been manufactured from precious stones. Unfortunately, the five arrowheads had been lost somewhere along their route.

Although Mendoza was intrigued by their reports, he wanted more information before taking any drastic steps, and he would move cautiously until he obtained it. The chief question he pondered was how he could best obtain it.

He decided that he would take a small gamble. At a negligible cost, he would send an exploring party north to investigate the situation, and he could think of no one better qualified to lead it than Cabeza de Vaca.

Cabeza de Vaca, however, had other plans. After nearly a decade of wandering and suffering untold ordeals in the wilderness, the riches he most desired were to return to Spain and a reunion with his wife, and to sit in his own patio in the soft light of the afternoon. He went home.

Nor was Castillo available. He had become enamored of a wealthy widow, and his future looked bright in Mexico. It was a very pleasant land, and he wanted to settle in it. Mendoza agreeably granted him an income from some Indian ranches, and Castillo was content.

Some accounts of the day relate that Dorantes, preparing to leave for Spain, gave Mendoza one of his most valuable possessions, Estevanico the Black. Other chronicles, however, intimate that there was more involved in the transaction than a mere gesture of friendship. The shrewd Mendoza was fully aware of Estevanico's ability as an explorer and wilderness ambassador, and understood, as well, the value of the training he had received as a pupil of the great Cabeza de Vaca. Moreover, the Viceroy had stated that in the event an investigation of the north should be made Estevanico would be "most useful for the purpose, he being an intelligent person." It would not have been strange, therefore, if Mendoza had asked that Estevanico be placed in his service. Dorantes would have been in no position to have refused such a request.

Whatever the case, Dorantes was in Vera Cruz in the spring of 1537 waiting to sail for Spain when Mendoza sent him a message asking him to return to Mexico City for a conference. Dorantes went back, and Mendoza proposed that he undertake the northern exploration. Estevanico would go with him. Reluctantly Dorantes agreed.

Mendoza furnished the necessary money, men and supplies. When all was in readiness, the unhappy Dorantes had enough courage to announce that he had changed his mind, and did not care to go on the journey.*

Mendoza eventually forgave Dorantes and held him in high esteem, but at the time he was thoroughly exasperated with him. He had thought, he reported to the King, that Dorantes "might render a great service to your Majesty if I should send him with forty or forty-five horsemen and all the things necessary to explore that country. I have spent a great amount of silver for the expedition, but for reasons unknown to me the affair has come to naught."

Besides appropriating several thousand Royal pesos, assigning a number of soldiers, and buying equipment, Mendoza had sent orders to officials in Culiacán to assemble a number of Indians who had followed Cabeza de Vaca on the march along the west coast. It was his thought that inasmuch as these natives knew that Dor-

---

* However, Dorantes did not return to Spain. Like Castillo, he decided to remain in Mexico, and he, too, married a widow with a substantial income from rental properties.

antes and Estevanico could be trusted they would be valuable as emissaries in the march through the unknown northern wilderness.

Now all these plans had gone awry. Informing the King of the situation, Mendoza lamented that, after all the preparations he had made, only Estevanico was left to lead the expedition. And that could not be done. A Negro slave, regardless of his ability, trustworthiness and experience, could not be placed in command of an exploring party. If Indians would loyally serve him, Spanish soldiers would resent his authority, and not only might refuse to obey him in the wilderness but might well dispose of him with a timely shot in the back.

Moreover, Estevanico was a Moor and not a Christian. It was probably that thought which caused Mendoza to take a new course in the struggle toward a solution of his dilemma. Numerous padres had been fearless explorers and skillful diplomats to the Indians. They went into the wilderness armed only with messages of hope and the word of God, whereas soldiers carried deadly weapons and were not averse to using them. If he could find a friar with the required courage and zeal . . . Fate chose to resolve Mendoza's problem for him.

At precisely the right moment a well-known missionary, called Fray Marcos de Niza, appeared in Mexico City. For seven years, submitting to a craving for adventure and sightseeing, Fray Marcos had roamed the New World. He had been in Santo Domingo, Guatemala and South America. After witnessing the destruction of Peru and Ecuador, he had protested strongly to Bishop Zumárraga of Mexico City about the cruelties inflicted on the natives of those two countries. In reply, the Bishop had asked him to come to the Mexican capital and prepare written reports for submission to the authorities in Spain. Fray Marcos had complied promptly, and had arrived early in 1537.

He was presented to Mendoza, who was as shocked by his accounts as the Bishop. It did not take the Viceroy long to realize that Fray Marcos was just the man he wanted for the northern venture, a man of courage, with wilderness experience, who was physically strong, possessed of a great imagination, and brimming with ardor and optimism. The Bishop agreed, recommending Fray Marcos in the highest terms and describing him as "reliable, of approved virtue and fine religious zeal." Another high Church official added the testimonial that the peripatetic missionary was also "skilled in cosmography and in the arts of the sea, as well as in theology."

Mendoza needed nothing more. He wrote to the Spanish Sovereign for permission to send Fray Marcos, with Estevanico as a guide, on a scouting expedition to the north.

In view of future events, one may wonder how well, if at all, Mendoza understood that inseparably linked with Fray Marcos's imagination, ardor, optimism, zeal and enthusiasm were two other pronounced characteristics: talent as a promotor and the ability to dramatize himself and everything he did. Mendoza may have been astute enough to realize that he possessed such gifts. If he did not, he soon became fully and unhappily aware of the fact.

Approval of Mendoza's proposal came from King

Charles V in the fall of 1538. Matters were shaping up to Mendoza's satisfaction. Another padre, Fray Onarato, Estevanico, a group of northern Indians, and some slaves would go with Fray Marcos on the journey. As it would not be necessary to send any soldiers, no one would have to be paid, and the cost of equipment and supplies would be small. Mendoza was gratified that he would not, after all, endanger his own good record with expenditures of the King's money on a scheme he was not convinced would turn out to be profitable.

In August, 1538, Mendoza had appointed a young nobleman Governor of the new west coast Province of Nueva Galicia, which contained some of the settlements the deposed Guzmán had founded. The twenty-eight year old Governor was Don Francisco Vásquez de Coronado.

As Fray Marcos and his motley contingent would start from Nueva Galicia on their northern scout, Coronado, who was preparing to leave Mexico City for his new post, was instructed by Mendoza to aid the party in getting under way. He should see that they were properly equipped, and take them under his protection as far as Culiacán. It was not an obligation unwelcome to Coronado. His own dreams of conquest and acquiring riches for both his country and himself were no less fervid than those of Mendoza, or, for that matter, any conquistador in New Spain.

In the fall of 1538 a brilliant procession of soldiers, gentlemen adventurers, Indian servants, and herds of livestock crawled on its way over the high rocky road that ran out of the Valley of Mexico to Guadalajara and

Accompanied by Fray Marcos and Fray Onarato, Estevanico the Black set out to find the Seven Cities.

on to the distant Pacific Coast. At its head rode the new Governor of Nueva Galicia.

In the wake of the column trudged a group which in appearance contrasted drastically with the splendor and ostentation of Coronado and his military escort. No armor glistened in the sun, no plumes or banners waved, in the little company. Behind the strapping, ebony Estevanico paddled the two friars, Marcos and Onarato, clad in robes of dusty Zaragosa cloth. After them came a score of half-naked Indians charged with their personal bundles and the few articles of equipment which would go with them on their journey into the unknown north.

So began, on that day in the fall of 1538, one of the greatest adventure stories in the history of the New World.

4 / THE DISOBEDIENT MOOR

Spring was in its full glory when the two friars, Estevan-ico, and a group of Indians set out on foot from Culiacán on their mission to the north. The day was Friday, March 7, 1539.

The written instructions which the Viceroy Mendoza had sent to Fray Marcos were long and detailed. The Indians encountered were to be assured that they need no longer fear slave hunters. Spaniards who mistreated Indians would be punished. All natives who demonstrated their loyalty to the King would be rewarded. The Viceroy was very specific in telling Fray Marcos what to look for on the journey, saying: "You shall be very careful to observe the number of people that there are, whether they are few or many, and whether they are scattered or living together. Note also the nature, the fertility and climate of the land; the trees, plants and domestic and wild animals there may be; the character of the country, whether it is broken or flat; the rivers, whether they are large or small; the stones and metals which there are; and of all things that be sent or brought, send or bring samples of them in order, that his Majesty may be informed of everything."

Mendoza apparently favored the popular conception that North America consisted of two narrow isthmuses between two oceans, for he ordered Fray Marcos to "endeavor always to learn if there is any information about the seacoast, both the North and South Seas, for it may be that the land narrows and that a sea inlet reaches the interior of the land . . . leave letters buried at headlands, at the foot of some tree outstanding for its size . . . Mark the tree with a cross . . . Likewise, at the mouths of rivers and suitable harbors, on prominent trees near the water, make the same sign, a cross, and leave letters . . . if I send ships they will be advised to look for this sign." Thus, it became known that Mendoza already was thinking about sending a sea expedition to solve the northern mystery.

The Viceroy's next words suggest he held private hopes that Fray Marcos would make important discoveries. He told the friar: "Send back reports with the utmost secrecy so that appropriate steps may be taken without disturbing anything, because in the pacification of what is discovered the services of our Lord and the welfare of our natives shall be taken into consideration." In other words, serving the Lord and protecting the natives were handy reasons for secrecy, until the value of the discoveries, such as gold mines and mountains of jewels, could be thoroughly secured for the Royal government and would not fall into the hands of unscrupulous conquistadors.

Regarding Estevanico, Mendoza commanded that he obey Fray Marcos, and should he fail to carry out all orders the friar gave him, Estevanico "will be at fault and incur the penalties falling on those who disobey the persons empowered by his Majesty to command them." These were strong words for such a commonplace issue. Slaves were not in the habit of being disobedient, and ordinarily a threat in the name of the King was not needed to hold them in line. Obviously Mendoza understood that Estevanico was not only strong-willed but possessed qualities of leadership and determination, and that, unlike other slaves, he was not fearful of asserting himself.

Mendoza was right. Estevanico had no intention of obeying anyone. He fully realized that once they were in the wilderness, beyond the reach of the military, the friars would be completely dependent upon him for their survival. He would be the one who would make decisions, and he relished the thought of being in such an influential position. His conferences with Mendoza had inflated his ego. What other slave ever had been given such consideration, and called intelligent, by a Viceroy? If he was not in name commander of the expedition, he was in fact. He had been over the trail as far as Pueblo de los Corazones. He was the man the Indians knew, and their trust would be in him. No longer would he be overshadowed by the great Cabeza de Vaca. Now he would be a god in his own right.

In preparing for the journey, Estevanico had acquired considerable baggage, clothing, ornaments, a tent, warm sleeping robes, and other articles he felt a man of his high station properly should possess. Among his personal belongings were four large green pottery dinner plates. On them he was ceremoniously served each meal, and he permitted no one else to use them. His food was prepared according to his directions, and it consisted of the finest wilderness delicacies his retinue of servants was able to obtain for him. Someone—perhaps Coronado or another high official—had presented him with two greyhounds, and the noble animals trotted obediently beside him.

In one of his packs was a sacred medicine rattle made from a gourd. It was one of several which had been given to Cabeza de Vaca by Indians in west Texas. Medicine rattles were among the most highly revered possessions of the peoples whom the four strange men had met on their long journey across the continent. The story of Estevanico's life, however, might well have had a different ending, and the story of the discovery of the American Southwest undoubtedly would have been different, if he had not taken the gourd rattle with him.

The first serious setback of the expedition occurred at Petatlán on the Sinaloa River. Fray Onarato was taken seriously ill, and after a delay of three days it became apparent that he could not continue. Fray Marcos ordered that he be carried back to Culiacán, some sixty leagues behind them, on a litter.* Saying a sad farewell

* The Spanish judicial league equaled 2.634 English miles. Fray Onarato would recover and resume his religious duties in Compostela.

Estevanico made many friends among the Indians and enjoyed taking part in their dances and ceremonies.

to his companion, Fray Marcos "guided by the Holy Spirit"—but also by Estevanico—resumed the journey.

Indians are popularly pictured as being always solemn, stoical and expressionless. Nothing could be more untrue. They love fun, clever pantomime, revelry and story-telling. They laugh uproariously at practical jokes, and like nothing better than to sing and dance. Estevanico's gay manner, his willingness to join them in ceremonials and social festivities were highly appreciated, and his forceful and dominating personality evoked their admiration and attracted them to him.

In his *Relación,* Cabeza de Vaca made it clear that Estevanico was welcomed, respected and genuinely liked by Indians. There had been occasions, however, when Estevanico's brashness with Indian women had brought objections from their husbands, and Cabeza de Vaca had been forced to be stern with him. It had been Cabeza de Vaca's belief that the role of "men from the sun" was better played in discreet silence, and through reservation and detachment. Familiarity and sociability, he thought, would tend to lower them to the level of ordinary men in the eyes of the Indians. He had counseled his companions to remain aloof, never cold, unfriendly or disdainful, but never going to the extreme of being patronizing or purposefully amiable and engaging in small talk. Castillo and Dorantes had shared this attitude, but Estevanico had not.

The Moor had seen no reason to restrain or conceal the natural urges he possessed. Yet, for the most part he had complied with Cabeza de Vaca's admonitions because he respected him. He understood that Cabeza de Vaca's capacity for leadership was greater than his own or that of the others. Moreover, he wanted to live as much as anyone. So for the most part he had been circumspect, but not without protest, and Cabeza de Vaca had left no doubt of his own appreciation of the Moor's loyalty and devotion and his capability as an explorer.

Now there was no Cabeza de Vaca. There was only a devout, sober-faced friar with inflexible and narrow morality to command him, and Estevanico did not propose to be restrained with strictness he considered unnecessary. He marched on, doing almost exactly as he pleased.

The group reached Vacapa, in the present State of Sinaloa, late in March, and Fray Marcos decided to remain until after Easter. It was there that he made the decision which so suddenly changed the expedition from what might well have been a triumph into a tragedy. While he gave himself to Easter devotions, he told Estevanico to go on ahead "to see whether, by that route, information could be obtained of what we were seeking." The statement is notable more for its omissions than for what it says.

The truth was that although Estevanico was doing a most competent job as a guide, Fray Marcos had become deeply disturbed by his actions and his conduct. Despite his strong disapproval, Estevanico ignored him and swaggered through heathenish medicine ceremonies, made the sign of the cross over sick Indians, danced and sang with them through the night, and drank the vile

Indian stimulants. Estevanico refused to adhere to Fray Marcos's demand that he refuse the turquoises and corals and countless other gifts proffered by the natives. In fact, Estevanico had no hesitancy in asking for any article which attracted his eye, and in Fray Marcos's view he was acquiring a greater fortune than any slave properly should possess.

There was more than that to the matter. For a time Fray Marcos had held the hope that his guide would grow weary of his carousing, dancing, drinking and sacrilegious performances. At last he had become convinced that was not to be the case, and he had concluded that the entire venture might be better served if he let the irrepressible Moor go ahead. At least he would be less embarrassed and discord would be avoided. If Estevanico got into trouble, it might be just as well to let him get out of it by himself in the best way he could.

Under the orders Fray Marcos gave him, Estevanico was to advance no more than fifty or sixty leagues. The friar wrote: "I arranged with him that should he learn of some inhabited and rich country—something really important—he should not go any farther but return in person or send me Indians bearing the following sign: If it were something moderate, he should send me a white cross a span in size; if it were of greater importance, he should send me one two spans in size; and if it were something better and greater than New Spain, he should send me a large cross."

Estevanico had been gone only four days when several Indians arrived in Vacapa and astonished Fray Marcos by presenting him with a cross the size of a man. One of them brought the padre a message. It was that Estevanico had met people who had seen great cities in the north. "This person," Fray Marcos reported, "told me of so many marvels of the land that I postponed believing them until after seeing them or having further verification. He told me that it was thirty days' travel from the place where Esteban was to the first city of the land, which is called Cibola."

Fray Marcos added that the courier also said "that in the first province there are seven very large cities, all under one ruler, with large houses of stone and lime, all joined in an orderly manner, and the ruler's house is four stories high. The doors have many decorations of turquoises, of which there is a great abundance, and the people are very well clothed. There are other provinces farther on, each one of which he claims to be much more important than these seven cities. I rendered thanks to our Lord."

Now the cities believed for so long to exist somewhere in the New World had a new name—the Seven Cities of Cibola. But were they truly the seven cities of the old legend? Fray Marcos was ready to leave Vacapa to learn the truth when a second cross the size of the man arrived. With it came a message from Estevanico: "Hurry."

In a state of great excitement, Fray Marcos left Vacapa two days after Easter Sunday. He soon reached the Indian villages from which the crosses had been sent, and where the Moor had promised to wait for him. Estevanico had gone.

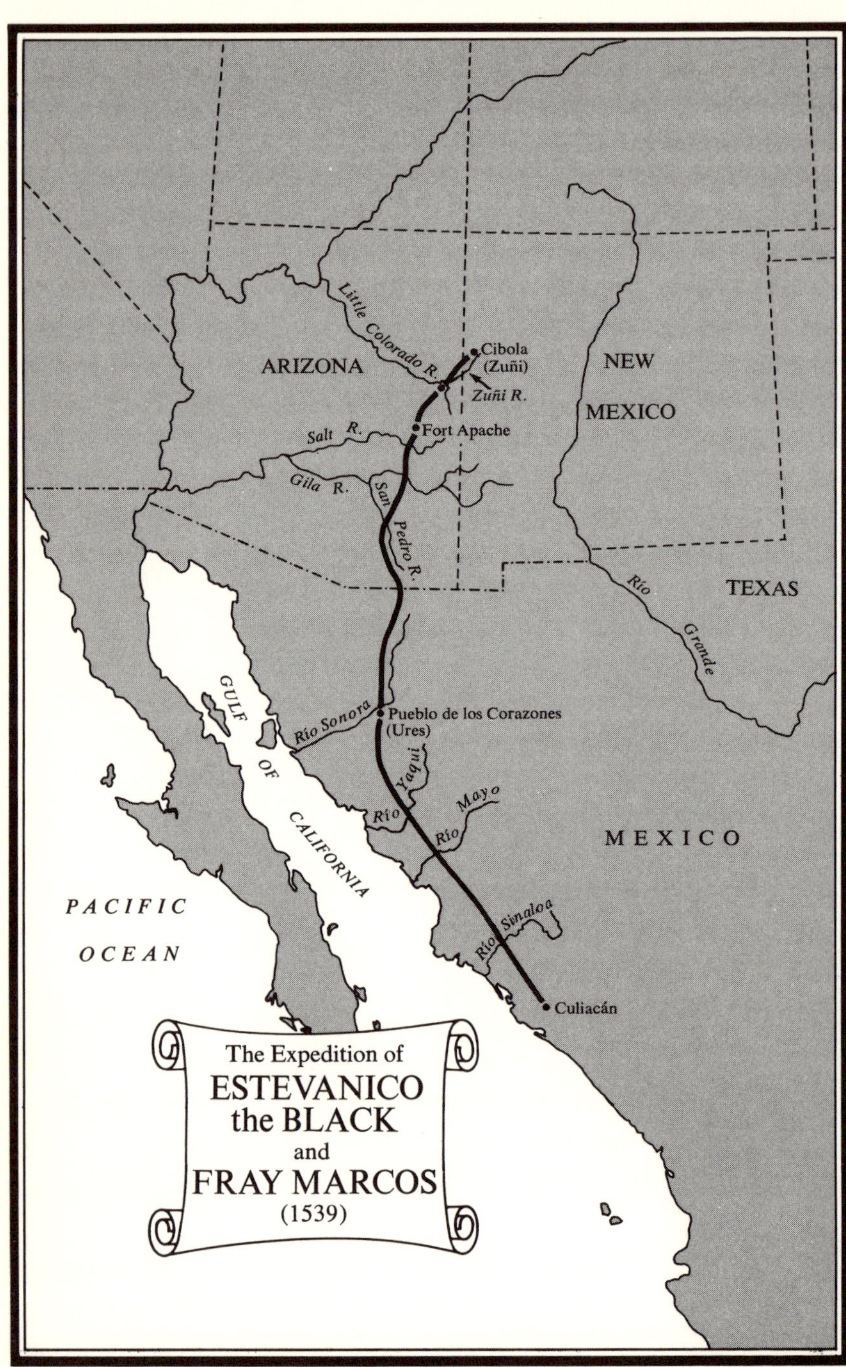

Little Colorado R.
ARIZONA
Cibola (Zuñi)
NEW
MEXICO
Zuñi R.
Salt R.
Fort Apache
Gila R.
San Pedro R.
TEXAS
Río Grande
GULF OF CALIFORNIA
Río Sonora
Pueblo de los Corazones (Ures)
Yaqui
Río Mayo
Río
MEXICO
PACIFIC OCEAN
Río Sinaloa
Río
Culiacán
The Expedition of
ESTEVANICO
the BLACK
and
FRAY MARCOS
(1539)

Now began one of the strangest and most notable chases in American history. Day after day in April and May Fray Marcos attempted to overtake Estevanico, and in every village he reached he received word that Estevanico was not far ahead. Profoundly exasperated, he plodded on. Other messengers arrived to tell him that Estevanico would wait for him in a certain place, but when he had reached that place the result was always the same: Estevanico had gone.

Castañeda wrote that Estevanico kept ahead of Fray Marcos because he "thought he could get all the reputation and honor himself, and that if alone he should discover those settlements with such famous high houses, he would be considered bold and courageous."

It was true that Estevanico wanted wealth, honor and fame, but he was not entirely disloyal to Fray Marcos. He opened the way so that Fray Marcos might travel in complete safety, and the priest admitted that as he pushed on in hot pursuit of his disobedient guide he always received good lodging and a friendly reception. He had no reason to complain about the job Estevanico was doing as an advance man.

At last he received a message that Estevanico would wait for him at Pueblo de los Corazones. Fray Marcos redoubled his efforts, making an exhausting march to the City of the Hearts. Estevanico had changed his mind, however, and had departed only a day or two earlier. Weary and worn, Fray Marcos rested a few days before starting on in pursuit of the scoundrelly, maddening Moor.

Now the trail passed through country that had never been entered by a European, white or black. Estevanico was leading the way into a land that was a blank space on the maps of the world, a land known only to the few Indians who lived in it or who passed through it on trading missions. Fray Marcos sent frantic pleas to Estevanico to wait, but he was never to see him again.

5 / DEATH AT HAWIKUH

A wild and beautiful procession wound its way over the ancient Indian trading trail that ran northward from Pueblo de los Corazones and out of the valley of the Río Sonora. Surrounding Estevanico were three hundred Indians, all dressed in their finest clothing and wearing their most valuable possessions.

Estevanico had adorned himself in a manner he thought appropriate for the march of discovery. His powerful legs and arms were decorated with clusters of bright feathers. A crown of plumes accentuated his height. Little bells tinkled merrily on his ankles. Strings of turquoise and coral dripped over his big chest. He strode with vigor, his keen eyes constantly searching the vast sweeps of rugged country that reached away on every side to hazy horizons. Always near him, prepared to carry out any command he might give, was Bartolomé, a native of Petatlán, and his chief aide.

In a few days the Mexican mountains had been left

behind and the trail twisted on through a vast *despo-blado,* a desolate region in which few people lived. The Indians knew the way, however, since many of them had made the journey several times. They knew the locations of the little streams and waterholes, and they had prepared well for the ordeals that must be overcome. Steadily onward the colorful column crawled, across the angular tilted mesas, up the hot valleys, over high ridges and sweeping plains, through the canyons.

With each stride Estevanico the Black wrote history in the dust, and on a May day in the year 1539 he entered the region that would become the Southwest of the United States. After crossing the divide which separates the Mexican State of Sonora and the American State of Arizona, the trail he followed went down the San Pedro River. He passed the sites of the present communities of Hereford, Charleston, Fairbank and Saint David. In the vicinity of Benson, his guides led him toward the northeast, across Arivipai Valley, to Eagle Pass, the opening between the Santa Teresa and Pinaleño Mountains. Here was the old Indian ruin called Chichilticale [Red House], and near it the trail once more turned northward. Reaching the Gila River it went on across high plateau country to the Little Colorado River, in the vicinity of St. Johns. Turning northeasterly again, it crossed Carrizo Creek and reached the Zuñi River, which came out of Cibola.

The goal was not far off now. The procession continued up the Zuñi River, and one day from a rise Estevanico saw, beyond the vast undulating sweep, the walls of the first city of Cibola. The Indians told him it was called Hawikuh.

On the long march from Culiacán Estevanico had followed a custom practiced by Cabeza de Vaca of sending a significant token or symbol ahead to each Indian village through which he would pass. The purpose was to assure the inhabitants that he was approaching in friendship and that they need have no fear. As he gazed at distant Hawikuh, he dispatched several Indian messengers to announce his arrival. With them he sent the sacred medicine rattle he had brought from Mexico City. To it he had attached some small bells and two feathers, one red and one white.

The Indians who lived in the Pueblo of Hawikuh were Zuñis. If they had heard of white men, which was not impossible, it was certain they had never seen one. It is even more certain they had never seen a black man. Word that white and black men existed might have reached them from two directions over trading routes. They might have learned that Cabeza de Vaca and his companions had visited the pueblos of the Jumanos on the Río Grande. They might have heard from Opatas that the same four men had been in Pueblo de los Corazones and other towns when on their way to Mexico City. Indeed, it is logical to believe that they did know that human beings of a strange breed, or breeds, had come out of the East, and that others of a similar kind had captured slaves in northern Mexico. Such exciting news would have traveled fast and far in the wilderness, most likely carried by traders from tribe to tribe.

The messengers sent to Hawikuh soon returned badly frightened. They had presented the gourd rattle and had delivered Estevanico's message that he came in peace to the Zuñis. After examining the rattle, the head chief had hurled it to the ground in great anger and had told the messengers to leave at once, "for he knew what sort of people they represented, and they should tell them not to enter the city or he would kill them all."

Estevanico had laughed. The same thing had happened more than once when he had been with Cabeza de Vaca. There was nothing to fear, for always before Indians who had been unfriendly at first had been humble and hospitable in the end.

Confidently and boldly Estevanico went on to Hawikuh. When he came to the entrance to the pueblo he found the Zuñis armed and arrayed in battle lines. Suddenly they rushed upon him and he was overwhelmed and taken prisoner. Castañeda wrote that Estevanico was taken into a "little hut they had outside their village, and the older men and the governors heard his story and took steps to find out the reason he had come to that country. For three days they made inquiries about him and held a council." Estevanico told his questioners that white men were coming behind him "who were sent by a great Lord, and knew about the things in the sky, and how these were coming to instruct them in divine matters."

The Zuñis headmen did not swallow the tale. Above all else, one thing convinced them that Estevanico was lying. They could not bring themselves to believe that "people were *white* in the country from which he came and that he was sent by them, he being *black*." To the Zuñis this was utterly unreasonable. Estevanico was a spy "from some nations who wished to come and conquer them." They decided to kill him. To prove to themselves that he was not a man from the sky or a god, as he claimed, after they killed him they cut him up in little pieces.

Fray Marcos and the Opatas guiding him were still several days' march from Hawikuh when an Indian runner brought them word that Estevanico had been slain. Soon two more couriers appeared, and the priest wrote that they "confirmed the unhappy news that Esteban, and all those who were with him, who numbered more than three hundred men, besides many women, had been killed by those of Cibola, and only they had escaped . . . I thought I should be lost. I feared not so much to lose my life, as not to be able to return and report on the greatness of the country."

Fray Marcos asserted that the leaders of the Indians with him, fearing that they too would be killed, wanted to turn back. At last, after giving them all his possessions, he was able to persuade them to go on with him.

He admitted that he had not entered Hawikuh, but claimed that he had observed it from a distant hilltop. He reported that the land was "the greatest and best of all that had been discovered," and that Hawikuh "has a fine appearance, the best I have seen in these regions . . . The city is larger than the city of Mexico."

The absurdity of this assertion, of course, would soon

Afraid to venture into Hawikuh, Fray Marcos claimed
he had seen an impressive city from a distance.

be established. After taking possession of the Province of Cibola in the name of the King, Fray Marcos turned about and fled, as he said, "with more fear than food," back to Mexico.*

It was near the end of June when he reached Governor Coronado at Compostela and gave him an account of the northern mission and the death of Estevanico. According to Castañeda, Fray Marcos told Coronado "such great things about what the Negro Esteban had discovered and what they had heard from the Indians, and about other things they had heard about the South Sea and islands and other riches, that, without stopping for anything, the governor set off at once for the City of Mexico, taking Friar Marcos with him, to tell the viceroy about it." Coronado "made the things seem more important by not talking about them to anyone except his particular friends, under promise of the greatest secrecy, until after he had reached Mexico and seen Don Antonio de Mendoza. Then it began to be noised abroad that the Seven Cities . . . already had been discovered."

The word was out: the Seven Cities had been found. Mexico City, from the Viceroy's palace to the lowest slave quarters, was in a state of wild excitement.

* There is ample evidence indicating that Fray Marcos never saw Hawikuh. Indeed, it is unlikely that he got within three or four days' journey of it. Some scholars have suggested that his statements were the result of mistakes he made in interpreting signs and gestures made by his Indian guides—a very generous view of the matter. Other historians, however, hold the opinion that they were pure fabrications designed to enhance his own reputation as a courageous explorer. Subsequent events, as well as reports by Coronado, Castañeda and others, give strong support to the latter conclusion.

A great new expedition, of which Coronado would be the Captain-General, was being organized by the Viceroy. Fray Marcos would go with it in command of a contingent of priests who would establish missions and convert the northern Indians to Christianity. Noblemen, gentlemen adventurers, military officers, and dreamers, wealthy and poor alike, pleaded with Coronado to let them go with him. Many agreed to pay all their own expenses, with the understanding, of course, that they would share in the treasures obtained.

Fray Marcos thoroughly enjoyed being in the spotlight. He was hailed as a hero wherever he went. His original glowing report to Coronado and Mendoza about Cibola got better with repetition until it was almost beyond belief. Word had soon spread to Cuba and other places outside Mexico that a new world had been discovered. In Havana a traveler swore under oath that Fray Marcos had told him Cibola "is a land rich in gold, silver and other wealth, and has great cities; the houses are of stone, and terraced like those of Mexico; the people have weights and measures, and are civilized. They marry only once, wear woolen clothes, and ride about on some animals whose name he does not know."

Fabulous stories, however, came not only from prominent persons. For example, a Mexico City barber said that while he was shaving Fray Marcos, the padre, being in a chatty mood, had told him through the lather that in Cibola there were "many walled cities guarded by gates. The people were rich, the women even wearing belts made of gold. In the country there were silversmiths, blacksmiths, slaughterhouses, baths, sheep and partridges."

Although the Viceroy Mendoza authorized the conquest and was willing to invest a large amount of money in it, his natural caution caused him to wonder whether Cibola truly was the marvelous country it had been made out to be by Fray Marcos. After the arrival of Cabeza de Vaca and his companions, he had sent the friar and Estevanico to investigate the situation in the north. The results had been encouraging, indeed, far more encouraging than he had expected. Still he was not satisfied.

He decided that while Coronado made preparations during the winter for the great expedition, he would send a small party, this time on horseback, to check on the report of Fray Marcos. The man he selected for the duty was Melchior Díaz, alcalde-mayor of Culiacán, an officer with many years' experience in the wilderness of the Pacific Coast. As Mendoza well knew, Díaz was a man of unquestionable integrity, thoroughly competent in dealing with Indians, and a realist who would not be taken in by tall tales. If the truth was obtainable, Díaz would get it, and would report accurately what he saw and learned, and nothing else.

It was mid-November of 1539, a poor time of the year to be starting north, when Díaz, with forty-five mounted soldiers and Indians, left Culiacán on the trail to Cibola. The mission of Díaz holds an important place in the history of American exploration, not because it was a daring venture and not because of Díaz's discoveries, but because he and his men were the first to take horses into any part of the vast territory that would become the western United States.

6 / DREAMS OF GLORY

With brilliant pageantry the great expedition of Coronado was marching north in the spring of 1540. On the right of the long parade was the great wall of the Sierra Madre, tier after tier and peak after peak, lifting its immensity under the blue haze of awesome heights, and on the left the shimmering Pacific reached away into illimitable distance. Three ships commanded by Hernando de Alarcón soon would leave to sail up the Gulf of California with additional equipment, munitions and supplies. Somewhere along the eastern shore of the gulf the land and sea forces would be united . . . or so it was planned.

In Coronado's colorful army were more than two hundred and fifty men on horseback, nearly a hundred foot soldiers (a few accompanied by their wives and children), several hundred Indian servants, camptenders and herdsmen, and half a dozen padres in robes and sandals led by the celebrated Fray Marcos. At the rear, stir-

Coronado's large, well-equipped expedition marched northward with hopes of finding treasure in Cibola.

ring up a great dust, came droves of cattle, sheep, and oxen, a long train of heavily loaded packmules, and a great herd of horses. It was a superbly equipped and mightily armed company. Many of the Spaniards, not a few of whom were gentlemen of high social position, were garbed in silks and fine cloth. Their armor glinted in the sunlight, and the plumes of their helmets waved haughtily in the breeze from the sea. The Indians, barefooted and bareheaded, wore hides and cotton protectors. They carried many types of weapons—guns, swords, lances, bows and arrows, javelins, slings, clubs— giving the column great power as a fighting force.

Although the way grew increasingly difficult, spirits remained generally high and the dreams of glories and treasures ahead remained intact until they reached Chiametla. There they met Melchior Díaz and his men returning from their reconnaissance to the north, and the story Díaz told Coronado was anything but encouraging.

Díaz had not reached Hawikuh. Winter had defeated him. As he had ridden north from Pueblo de los Corazones the weather had grown steadily colder. Several of his soldiers had died from exposure. Doggedly he had kept on, however, until he reached the ancient ruin at Chichilticale (northeast of Benson, Arizona), where he was halted by snow and extreme cold. He had spent several miserable weeks in a flimsy mat shelter, and then had started back. But he had not come empty-handed. At every opportunity he had talked with Indians, many of whom had been to Cibola, and some of whom had traveled with Estevanico and Fray Marcos. There was no doubt that Estevanico had been slain at Hawikuh. There was, however, considerable doubt about other things Fray Marcos had reported.

The padre had said the trail to Cibola was good and easily traversed; Díaz had found it extremely difficult and in places almost impassable. Although the pueblos, according to the Indians, were much as Fray Marcos had described them, it was apparent that they were not "great cities." Díaz had been able to learn nothing of such valuable things as emeralds, gold and silver. Indeed, not a single Indian with whom he had talked had even implied that the people of Cibola possessed any kind of metal. The Indians of the north had turquoises, although not as many as Fray Marcos said he saw.

Castañeda, a soldier with the Coronado expedition who would become one of its chief historians, said that Coronado attempted to keep Díaz's account secret but that "the bad news leaked out." Aware that Coronado and numerous others were deeply disturbed by what they had heard, Fray Marcos "cleared away these clouds, promising that what they would see should be good, and that he would place the army in a country where their hands would be filled, and in this way he quieted them so that they appeared well satisfied."

Their satisfaction did not last long. Travel over the trail between the Río Mayo and Pueblo de los Corazones was extremely slow and hazardous. Coronado wrote the Viceroy:

"We all marched cheerfully along a very difficult way, where it was impossible to travel without making a new road or repairing the one already there. This troubled the soldiers not a little because everything which the friar had said was found to be quite the reverse; for among other things he had said and declared was that the way would be plain and good . . . But the truth is that there are mountains which, however well the trail might be repaired, could not be crossed without great danger that the horses would fall over the cliffs. Indeed, it was so bad that many of the animals which your Lordship sent as food for the army were lost on this part of the route, because of the roughness of the rocks. The lambs and wethers lost their hoofs along the way, and most of those I had brought from Culiacán I left at the river Yaqui because they were unable to travel."

Several soldiers and Indians and a number of horses had died from the ordeals. Supplies were running low, and the men were weakened from hunger. The Indian villages had little surplus food, for crops had been poor in the previous year. The maize growing in the fields was not yet ripe.

The soldiers complained bitterly and denounced Fray Marcos, but something may be said in the priest's defense. It should not be forgotten, as the historian Herbert E. Bolton points out, that most of Coronado's men "were the merest tenderfeet. Fray Marcos, on the other hand, was a veteran on the trail, in Peru, in Central America, and in Mexico. Moreover he was an enthusiast. What to Coronado's novices looked hard, to him seemed easy. Quite apart from gold, Marcos saw a great harvest all around him—a harvest of souls. What he wrote about

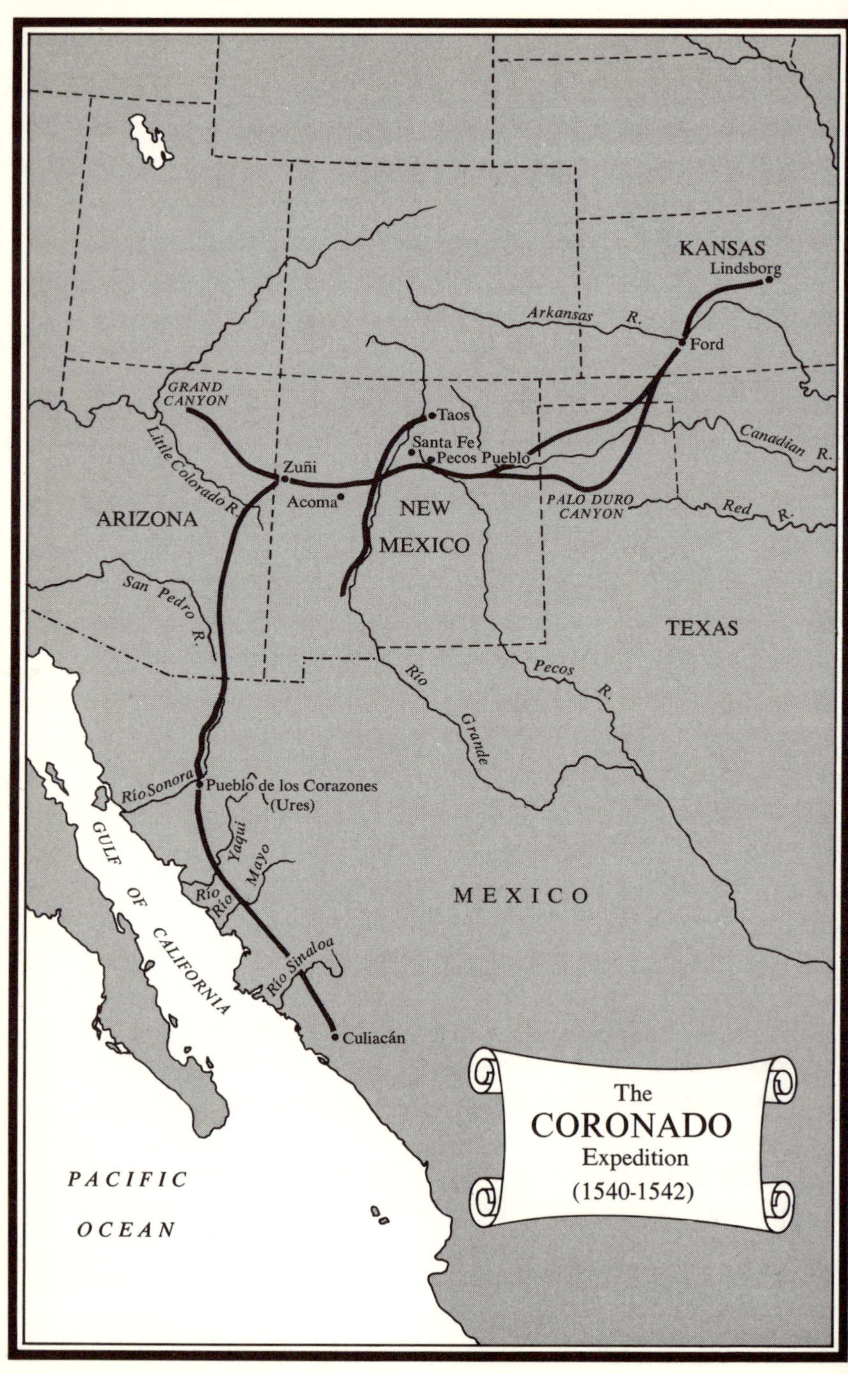

KANSAS
Lindsborg
Arkansas R.
Ford
GRAND CANYON
Little Colorado R.
Taos
Santa Fe
Pecos Pueblo
Canadian R.
Zuñi
Acoma
NEW MEXICO
PALO DURO CANYON
Red R.
ARIZONA
San Pedro R.
TEXAS
Río Grande
Pecos R.
Río Sonora
Pueblo de los Corazones
(Ures)
Río Yaqui
Río Mayo
MEXICO
GULF OF CALIFORNIA
Río Sinaloa
Culiacán
PACIFIC OCEAN
The
CORONADO
Expedition
(1540-1542)

treasure was for the encouragement of others. Aside from all this, it is to be remembered that, as he went through the country on his first expedition, Fray Marcos had been treated by the Indians (thanks to the good work of Estevanico) with the greatest care and tenderness."

With perhaps a hundred and twenty soldiers and a number of Indian servants Coronado went ahead of the main column, which, encumbered by baggage and animals, was forced to move at a slow pace. On the trip across the immense desert area north of the Sonora Valley the advance party suffered greatly because of a shortage of provisions and the exhausted condition of both men and horses. The combination of continual hardship and malnutrition took the lives of several more soldiers.

Where was the great city which Fray Marcos had said was larger than Mexico City? Did it exist at all? When, on a July day in 1540, they came within sight of Hawikuh, they knew that the answer was *no*.

Castañeda told how the bruised, weary and hungry men reacted as they gazed in bitter disappointment at the pueblo: ". . . such were the curses that some hurled at Friar Marcos that I pray God may protect him from them. It is a little, crowded village, looking as if it had been crumpled all up together. There are haciendas in New Spain which make a better appearance at a distance."

The Zuñis had been warned by scouts of Coronado's approach, and warriors had come from surrounding pueblos to help in the defense of Hawikuh. Several hundred fighters were concealed within the pueblo. Others were arrayed in battle formation before it. Coronado sent a small contingent of soldiers, priests and interpreters under Captain García López de Cárdenas to inform the Zuñis that he came in peace in the name of the King of Spain, and that they would suffer no injury if they, likewise, remained peaceful. When there was no response to these overtures, Cárdenas and his escort resorted to pantomime, placing their weapons on the ground and making signs to indicate that their intentions were not hostile.

The reply to this acting was a shower of arrows. Coronado rode up and made a second attempt to persuade the Cibolans to refrain from fighting. The result was the same, and several Spaniards and horses were wounded. "I did not wish them attacked," Coronado reported, "and although my men were begging me for permission, I enjoined them from doing so . . ." Actually, the Spaniards, worn and hungry, were not in condition to fight, and Coronado continued his efforts to induce the defenders to withdraw without further conflict.

The Cibolans only signaled the intruders to depart. "On the other hand," said Coronado, "when the Indians saw we did not move they took greater courage, and grew so bold that they came almost to the heels of our horses to shoot their arrows." The patience of starving men was short, and Coronado saw that "the time for hesitation had passed." The Spanish battlecry "Santiago!" was given, and Coronado led a charge.

Most of the Zuñis quickly retreated into the pueblo, which was built with a narrow, twisting entrance, and could be easily defended. The first assault failed, and the Spaniards abandoned their horses and launched another attack on foot. For nearly an hour the fighting raged. Coronado was wounded in the foot by an arrow and struck in the head with stones. He fell and was helped to safety. Cárdenas took command, and under him the soldiers began to break through the entrance of the town.

Suddenly the Cibolans made signs that they would surrender and asked permission to leave. Although Cárdenas replied that they might remain, they chose to go, and "they went away unharmed by the Spaniards." It was not blood the Spaniards wanted but food, and once they got into the pueblo they gorged themselves on "something we prized more than gold or silver; namely plentiful maize and beans, and turkeys." Days at ease followed. Amicable relations were established with the Cibolans through some of their leaders who accepted Coronado's invitation to confer with him, but the others remained in hiding in the surrounding country.

Up to this time the conquest had been a bleak disappointment and an extreme ordeal. As far as Coronado could learn, there were no great cities. The Province of Cibola consisted of seven pueblos, and the possessions of the people could hardly be called "treasures"—some turquoises, a few other semi-precious stones, buffalo robes and various kinds of skins.

But what lay beyond? The question burned in Coronado's thoughts. As far as Hawikuh he had followed a trail which had been traversed by others—by Estevanico and, in part at least, by Fray Marcos and Melchior Díaz. He had discovered nothing of value, but now he stood on the edge of country totally unknown to white men. What did it contain? How far did it go?

Coronado could be certain of only one thing: he did not intend to turn back without finding the answers to these questions. If he was discouraged, his great dream had not been destroyed. Yet, he was not impractical to the extent that he was blinded by visions or unfounded hopes. He faced a grim, and in some respects almost a desperate, situation. Of that he was painfully aware, and he understood that drastic steps had to be taken to relieve it.

He dispatched couriers to Mexico with urgent requests for supplies. From the Indians he learned that to the west was a great river, and this information gave rise to the hope that the ships commanded by Hernando de Alarcón might have reached it and were waiting there to hear from him. There was only one way to find out, and that was to send men to find them. This assignment was given to the reliable and experienced Melchior Díaz.

Coronado wasted no time in attempting to learn something of the country surrounding him. Indian leaders from distant towns responded to his calls to meet with him. From the information he gained in these councils, it seemed to him that a province to the north called Tusayán appeared to be most worthy of immediate investigation. He sent Captain Pedro de Tovar with a score of men to visit it.

Guided by Zuñis, Tovar and his soldiers followed a trail that skirted the amazing "forest of stone trees"— the Petrified Forest National Monument in Arizona. Their course took them on through country that today is part of the large Navajo Reservation. They were the first white men to see the famous Hopi towns, perched high on great mesas, which are now visited each year by thousands of travelers from all parts of the world.

The Hopis at first were inclined to fight the invaders, but after a brief skirmish, capitulated. From them Tovar learned that a big river did exist to the north and west. The Hopis offered to guide him to it, although the trail was difficult and there was little water on the way. Tovar, however, had orders to return after discovering Tusayán, and he started back to Hawikuh.

When he heard Tovar's report that the "great river of the west" could be reached from Tusayán, Coronado immediately sent another contingent to find it. This mission was commanded by Coronado's chief aide, Cárdenas, who took with him twenty-five mounted soldiers.

The Hopis willingly supplied Cárdenas with guides to show him the trail to the river, and on a September day in 1540 white men for the first time gazed into the awesome depths of one of the great scenic wonders of the world—the Grand Canyon.

"They spent three days on this bank [the south rim of the canyon]," Castañeda wrote, "looking for a passage down to the river, which looked from above as if the water was six feet across, although the Indians said it was half a league wide. It was impossible to descend, for after three days Captain Melgosa and one Juan Galeras and another companion, who were the three lightest and most agile men, made an attempt to go down at the least difficult place, and went down until those who were above were unable to keep sight of them. They returned about four o'clock in the afternoon, not having succeeded in reaching the bottom on account of the great difficulties which they found, because what seemed to be easy from above was not so, but instead very hard and difficult. They said they had been down about a third of the way and that the river seemed very large from the place that they reached, and that from what they saw they thought the Indians had given the width correctly. Those who stayed above had estimated that some huge rocks on the sides of the cliffs seemed to be about as tall as a man, but those who went down swore that when they reached these rocks they were bigger than the great tower of Seville [the famed bell tower of the Cathedral of Seville, which is 275 feet high]."

The Hopis made it clear to Cárdenas that the river at the bottom of the canyon eventually reached the sea (the Gulf of California), but that it could not be followed to its delta because of impassable deserts and canyons. Even there on the high South Rim there was insufficient water, and the Spaniards were forced "to go a league or two inland every day late in the evening in order to find water, and the guides said that if they should go four days farther it would not be possible to go on . . ."

Cárdenas had found the "great river of the west," the Colorado, that flowed into the Gulf of California, where it was hoped that Alarcón's supply ships were waiting, but it was impossible for him to follow it to the sea. All that he could do was turn back to Cibola, hoping that Melchior Díaz, who had been sent to look for the ships, would find them by taking a route that would lead him to the sea from Mexico.

With the discoveries of the Hopi towns and the Grand Canyon another large part of the darkness that enshrouded the north had been dispelled. Still nothing of value had been found. In a dispatch to Mendoza, Coronado lamented: "God knows I wish I had better news to write your Lordship, but I must tell you the truth . . . I must inform you of the bad as well as the good." He would, he told the Viceroy, continue to "suffer every hardship rather than abandon this enterprise; and to serve his Majesty if I can find any way to do so."

While Cárdenas was away, Coronado waited in Cibola for the arrival of the main part of his force, which was still moving slowly northward from the Sonora Valley. From Indians who visited him there, he learned of another large river to the east. He was told that near the river and along it were numerous towns and a large population. Farther on, said these visitors, were plains with great herds of wild cattle. The people to the east grew many crops and had bountiful supplies of meat and warm clothing. The Indians had described the upper Río Grande, the many pueblos of the river's environs, and the buffalo.

Coronado decided to send Captain Hernando de Alvarado, Fray Juan Padillo, and a small contingent of soldiers (twenty or possibly twenty-five went) to verify the reports that the country to the east was a land of plenty. When the main force arrived, it would be necessary to find winter quarters in which adequate supplies could be obtained. With orders to return within eighty days, Alvarado started from Hawikuh on August 29, 1540. He and his little group would be the first white men to penetrate New Mexico, cross the Río Grande (near the site of Albuquerque), and reach the Great Plains.

During Alvarado's absence, while the wondering and worried Coronado waited in Cibola, events of great importance were taking place far to the south and west.

With three supply ships, Alarcón had sailed north from Acapulco to the head of the Gulf of California. On the long voyage a constant lookout had been maintained for some signal from Coronado, but none had been received. Now, late in August, the vessels were anchored in dangerous shoal waters at the mouth of a great river. The pilots and seamen wanted to turn homeward, but Alarcón would not listen to them. He had been sent with supplies and equipment that were vital to Coronado, and he proposed to deliver them, if such an achievement were humanly possible. Perhaps the roaring river came from Cibola. He would find out.

Taking two small boats manned by the most able members of the ships' crews, Alarcón set out to fight the raging current of the river, to which he gave the name *Buena Guía*—Unfailing Guide. It was the Colorado, which passed in its long course from the far north through the Grand Canyon, and Alarcón and his sailors were the first Europeans to ascend it from its mouth.

They pushed upstream until they had passed the site of the present city of Yuma, Arizona. If the hundreds of Indians they encountered had never seen a white man, they knew of their existence. On September 1, Alarcón sat in council with headmen of a Yuman tribe who told him how Estevanico the Black had been killed and cut up in little pieces. Shortly afterward he heard from other natives that Coronado had invaded Cibola and had captured Hawikuh after a fight in which many persons had died.

Hawikuh, these people said, could not be reached by the river, but only by traveling for thirty days over great deserts. In vain Alarcón pleaded with them to guide him to it. They even refused to carry a message to Coronado, for word that more Spaniards were in the country would not be welcomed by the Cibolans. Any person bearing such unpleasant tidings would most probably suffer the same fate that had befallen Estevanico.

Faced with this hopeless situation, Alarcón turned back downstream. On the way he blazed a tree and buried letters in a jar at its foot—a message to tell whoever might follow him that he had been there and had done his best to complete the mission on which the Viceroy Mendoza had sent him. Then he sailed for Mexico. Another gateway to the Southwest had been opened.

In September, when Alarcón was still on the Colorado River, Melchior Díaz had set out from the valley of the

Río Sonora to carry out Coronado's orders to search for the supply ships. He took with him twenty-five cavalrymen and a number of Opata Indians as guides. The trail they followed crossed a region never before entered by white men, a region containing some of the most terrible deserts in the world. The path would later come to be known as the Devil's Highway, on which countless men and animals would perish.

Díaz reached the Colorado River, which he named *Río del Tizón* (Firebrand River), near its confluence with the Gila. Díaz was informed that Alarcón had been there only a few weeks before. Going downstream, Díaz found the blazed tree and the letters which told how Alarcón had tried in vain to get a message to Coronado and had gone back to Mexico.

After finding Alarcón's letters, Díaz explored the country west of the river—the land that would become American California. He was gravely wounded in a freakish accident a short distance south of the present border between Mexico and the United States. For three weeks his loyal men carried him on a litter in a desperate attempt to reach the Sonora Valley "in time for him to be confessed, for there was a priest there," but they lost the race. Díaz was buried somewhere along the Devil's Highway. His grave has never been found.*

Meanwhile, good news had come to Coronado at Hawikuh from the east. Two Pueblo Indian chiefs, Bigotes

---

* Full accounts of the courageous explorations of Alarcón and Díaz are contained in *The Discovery of California,* by the author of this book.

(Whiskers) and Cacique (Governor), had guided Alvarado through a bountiful land. In a report sent back by courier, Alvarado told Coronado of passing Acoma, the "Sky City," built atop a great mesa, and of more than eighty other pueblos, in which he had been received in friendship. He had been given all the food he and his soldiers required. He had given the name Nuestra Señora to the river that would later be called the Río Grande, writing that it "flows through a broad valley planted with fields of maize and dotted with cottonwood groves." At a place called Tiguex* there were twelve pueblos, six on each side of the river, and their inhabitants "seem to be good people, more devoted to agriculture than to war. They have a food supply of maize, beans, melons, and turkeys in great abundance. They clothe themselves in cotton, the skins of cattle [buffalo], and coats made of turkey feathers, and they wear their hair short." While he was at Tiguex "the Indians from the surrounding provinces came to offer me peace." The pueblos continued on for more than fifty leagues along the river, and Alvarado went north until he reached a very large town, which he called Braba. It was the famous pueblo later known as Taos. Returning downstream, Alvarado had turned east and had reached a great town that he described as "larger than any of the others and very strong. Its houses are four and five stories high, some of them being very fine. It has eight large patios, each with its corridor . . . it is fifteen leagues east of the river [Río Grande], and close to

* Near Bernalillo, New Mexico.

plains where the cattle roam." Alvarado was describing the enormous pueblo that stood on the Pecos River, on the ancient route Pueblo Indians followed to reach the buffalo herds, and the main east-west trading trail of the region. The Pecos Pueblo was the home of Alvarado's two guides, Bigotes and Cacique, and he and his soldiers were most hospitably received.

At Pecos Pueblo Alvarado came to know two young Indian men who would play important roles in the discovery of the Southwest. They were slaves who had been captured on the Great Plains by Bigotes and Cacique. The younger of the two, Ysopete, came from a place called Quivira, in a region that would become American Kansas. The other captive was a native of an area known as Harahey, which lay north of Quivira. The Spaniards nicknamed him Turk, because, as Castañeda said, "he looked like one."

Bigotes and Cacique asked to be relieved as guides, and Alvarado obtained the services of Ysopete and Turk to show him the way to the buffalo plains. The two captives were delighted with the assignment, for they hoped that it might enable them to escape and return to their homes. Four days after leaving Pecos Pueblo the explorers gazed out across the Great Plains of northeastern New Mexico. With Ysopete and Turk leading them, they descended a stream that later would be known as the Canadian River.

On the plains the Spaniards found a great herd of buffalo, and an account of the first buffalo hunt by Europeans in North America is contained in the chronicles of the Coronado Expedition. It describes the "wild cattle" as the "most monstrous beasts ever seen or read about. We availed ourselves of them, although with danger to the horses at first, until we had gained experience. There are such multitudes of them that I do not know what to compare them with unless it be the fish of the sea . . . the plains were covered with them. Their meat is as good as that of the cattle of Castile [Spain], and some said it was even better. The bulls are large and fierce, although they do not attack very often. But they have wicked horns and they charge and thrust savagely. They killed several of our horses and wounded many others." The Spaniards, thoroughly enjoying the sport, found that lances were the most effective weapons for killing running buffalo "and arquebuses [guns] when they are standing still."

By this time Turk was well aware that Alvarado was more interested in discovering treasure than in hunting buffalo, and he showed his cunning by concocting a fabulous tale. Instead of going east, he told the captain, Alvarado should turn to the northeast, for in his homeland were "gold, silver, fine fabrics and all manner of excellent food." Bigotes knew these things, declared Turk, for when he was captured he had in his possession a golden bracelet that Bigotes had taken from him.

Alvarado was interested, but the time allotted him for the mission was almost up, and he turned back to Pecos Pueblo. There he confronted Bigotes and Cacique and demanded the golden bracelet. They denied having it, and called Turk a liar. Enraged, Alvarado put them and

Turk and Ysopete in chains and took them with him. He would let Coronado decide who was lying.

As winter came to the high country of New Mexico Coronado and his advance guard, improperly clothed and not equipped to withstand the low temperatures in the open, united with Alvarado at the twelve pueblos of Tiguex on the Río Grande. The main force of the expedition was not far behind. At first the inhabitants of Tiguex were friendly and agreeably vacated some of their houses for the Spaniards, but trouble soon arose.

Castañeda told how the shivering soldiers, most of whom had been born and reared in hot countries, forced their way into homes and confiscated robes, cloaks, food, and anything else they desired, without giving "the natives a chance to consult about it . . . Thus, these people could do nothing except take off their own cloaks . . . which caused not a little hard feeling." The fires of "hard feeling" soon blazed into "open rebellion." The Spaniards' horse herd was attacked and several animals were killed. One of the pueblos was deserted. The gates of others were closed, and the people in them were prepared for battle.

After a council with his officers, Coronado issued orders to attack the pueblo called Arenal, which had been the scene of considerable trouble. He would make an example of it. None of the warriors were to be taken alive. Perhaps after it was subjugated the other people of Tiguex would remain peaceful and obedient.

Cárdenas was placed in command of the assault. It was launched, wrote Castañeda, "with so much surprise that they gained the upper story, with great danger, for they wounded many of our men from within the houses. Our men were on top of the houses in great danger for a day and a night and part of the next day, and they made some good shots with their crossbows and muskets. The horsemen on the plain with many of the Indian allies from New Spain smoked them out of the cellars . . . so that they begged for peace." Other Indians still holding out in the upper stories were told by soldiers on the roof that if they would surrender they would be pardoned. These defenders laid down their arms and emerged.

The offer of amnesty, however, had not been authorized by Cárdenas. Declaring that he had been ordered by Coronado "not to take them alive, but to make an example of them so that other natives would fear the Spanish," Cárdenas "ordered two hundred stakes to be prepared at once to burn them alive." When the Indians saw that the Spaniards intended "to bind them and roast them . . . they began to struggle and defend themselves with whatever was there and with the stakes they could seize . . . Our men who were on foot attacked . . . and then the horsemen chased those who escaped. As the country was level, not a man of them remained alive, unless it was some who remained hidden in the village and escaped that night to spread throughout the country the news that the strangers did not respect the peace they had made, which afterward proved a great misfortune. After this was over, it began to snow . . ."

Many of the Indians fled, but the battle of Tiguex was not over. As the year 1541 began, Coronado, who made his headquarters in the town of Alcanfor, was informed that a large number of warriors had begun to assemble at the Pueblo Moho and were fortifying it with the intention of continuing their defiance of the Spaniards. He ordered that they be driven out.

The attack on Moho, which stood on the west bank of the Río Grande and was the largest and strongest of the twelve Tiguex pueblos, quickly developed into a siege. The defenders of Moho rejected demands that they surrender, and Castañeda reported that Coronado "ordered the army to go and surround the village. He set out with his men in good order, one day, with several scaling ladders . . . he camped his force nearby, and then began the siege; but as the enemy had had several days to provide themselves with stores, they threw down such quantities of rocks upon our men that many of them were laid out, and they wounded nearly a hundred with arrows, several of whom afterward died on account of the bad treatment by an unskillful surgeon who was with the army."

For fifty days the soldiers attempted to break into Moho, but each assault was repulsed. Castañeda recounted: "The lack of water was what troubled the Indians most. They dug a very deep well inside the village, but were not able to get water, and while they were making it, it fell in and killed thirty persons. Two hundred of the besieged died in the fights [as well as a number of Spanish soldiers and gentlemen].

"One day . . . they asked to speak to us, and said that, since they knew we would not harm the women and children, they wished to surrender [them], because they were using up their water. It was impossible to persuade them to make peace, as they said the Spaniards would not keep an agreement made with them. So they gave us about a hundred persons, women and boys, who did not want to leave them."

The siege continued, but some of the defenders, including a number of women, "decided to leave the village one night, and did so . . . they started about the fourth watch, in the very early morning, on the side where the cavalry was. The alarm was given . . ." One Spaniard was killed and several were wounded, but the Indians were driven off "with great slaughter until they came to the river, where the water flowed swiftly and very cold. They threw themselves into this, and as the men had come quickly from the whole camp to assist the cavalry, there were few who escaped being killed or wounded.

"This ended the siege, and the town was captured . . ." *

---

* The original manuscript of Castañeda's narrative of the Coronado Expedition is not known to exist. However, a copy of it was made in Spain in 1596. A translation of this copy was made by Dr. George Parker Winship and published in 1896 by the Bureau of American Ethnology of Washington, D.C. It is from the Winship translation that the excerpts printed in this book have been taken.

7 / THE END OF
THE TRAIL

Throughout the cold and bloody winter Coronado had been haunted by the tales told by Turk. Now, in April, 1541, with spring in full bloom in the beautiful New Mexico country, he set off to verify them.

Having been a prisoner with a chain around his neck for several months had neither broken Turk's spirit nor dampened his imagination. When he was told that he and Ysopete, who also had been held a prisoner, would be taken along as guides, he spewed forth new tales more wondrous than those he previously had recited. Besides inconceivable amounts of gold and other treasures awaiting the taking in Quivira and Harahey, "there was a river in the level country which was two leagues wide, in which there were fishes as big as horses, and large numbers of very big canoes, with more than twenty rowers on a side, and that they carried sails, and that their lords sat on the poop under awnings, and on the prow they had a great golden eagle. He said also that the

76

lord of that country took his afternoon nap under a great tree on which were hung a great number of little gold bells, which put him to sleep as they swung in the air. He said also that everyone had their ordinary dishes made of wrought [silver] plate, and the jugs and bowls were of gold."

Coronado appeared to be almost hypnotized by Turk's babblings. He let the young booster of Quivira set the course to be followed. Now some soldiers, who obviously were less gullible, began to believe Turk was deceiving everyone, but if Coronado heard these opinions, he ignored them.

Turk had said that Quivira lay to the northeast, yet he led Coronado toward the southeast. Day after day the army crawled on across the vast Llano Estacado (Staked Plains), a country as flat and seemingly as endless as any on earth. In May they had reached a land that would become a part of the Panhandle of the State of Texas. They had now passed the point Alvarado had reached on his previous excursion to the "cattle country." For the first time Coronado himself was exploring territory never before entered by white men.

Castañeda, Juan de Jaramillo and other soldier-chroniclers of the expedition later wrote invaluable descriptions of the Great Plains and of the people dwelling on them at the very beginning of the period of recorded history. The first Indians they encountered were called Querechos. They were plains Apaches. Later the explorers met a people known as Tejas, and it was from this designation that the name Texas was derived.

So flat was the Llano Estacado that the Spaniards saw no hillock "which was three times as high as a man." The country was "like a bowl, so that when a man sits down, the horizon surrounds him all around at the distance of a musket shot." The Indians "travel like the Arabs, with their tents and troops of dogs loaded with poles and having Moorish packsaddles with girths. When the load gets disarranged, the dogs howl, calling some one to fix them right.

"These people eat raw flesh and drink blood. They do not eat human flesh.* They are a kind people and not cruel. They are faithful friends. They are able to make themselves very well understood by means of signs."

Of all the Indians in North America, as later explorers and frontiersmen would learn, the people of the Great Plains excelled in talking in the sign language, which combined beauty and fluid grace with great practicality. A conversation between plains Indians who were experts in it was nothing less than poetry in motion. It was a gesture communication that hardly fell short of a spoken language. It remained, of course, in the pantomime state, but those who could talk fluently in it could speak on any subject. They could talk clearly about hunting, war, personal experiences, the weather, domestic problems, troublesome relatives. They could recite history and legends, tell humorous and tragic stories, and they could speak to their gods. The Querechos, said Castañeda, by means of signs "made themselves under-

* Some tribes of Texas practiced cannibalism as a part of their religious ritual.

stood so well that there was no need of an interpreter." This assertion should be modified with the note that Coronado had with him two guides, Turk and Ysopete, who were competent talkers in the sign language.

The Querechos and Tejas dried the buffalo meat "in the sun, cutting it thin like a leaf, and when dry they grind it like meal to keep it . . . A handful thrown into a pot swells up so as to increase very much. They season it with fat, which they always try to secure when they kill a cow.* They empty a large gut and fill it with blood, and carry this around the neck to drink when they are thirsty. When they open the belly of a cow, they squeeze out the chewed grass and drink the juice that remains behind, because they say that this contains the essence of the stomach. They cut the hide open at the back and pull it off at the joints, using a flint as large as a finger, tied in a little stick, with as much ease as if working with a good iron tool . . . The quickness with which they do this is something worth seeing . . . There are great numbers of wolves on these plains, which go around with the cows . . . The rabbits, which are very numerous, are so foolish that those on horseback killed them with their lances."

In telling of how the Spanish soldiers confiscated some buffalo robes from the Tejas, Castañeda significantly remarked that the Indian "women and even some of the men wept, because they thought the army would not take anything, but would merely say a blessing over the

---

* This was *pemmican.*

goods, as Cabeza de Vaca and Dorantes had done when they passed that way."

The army was then in the area of Palo Duro Canyon, the great fissure which splits open the plains of the Texas Panhandle. Had Cabeza de Vaca and his three companions traveled that far north? Castañeda said nothing more about the matter, but Jaramillo supplied an explanation that resolved the mystery. An old Tejas Indian who had become blind "gave us to understand by signs that, many days before, he had met four others of our people near there but closer to New Spain . . . Thus, we understood and assumed them to be Dorantes, Cabeza de Vaca, and the others . . ."—Castillo and Estevanico the Black. The Tejas wandered over an immense area, and the meeting with Cabeza de Vaca had taken place farther to the south.

It will be remembered, too, that Cabeza de Vaca had called Indians he met on the Río Grande "the Nation of the Cows," because periodically they traveled northeastward to the Great Plains to hunt buffalo. Had Coronado encountered them on one of their hunts? Probably the answer to that question will never be known, but the fact remains that, six years before Coronado arrived, in those enormous plains of western Texas they had met the four men, three white and one black who had "come out of the sky."

On several occasions Ysopete had charged that Turk was leading the expedition astray. As far as the Texas Panhandle, Coronado's faith in Turk had remained unshaken, but at last he, too, began to suspect that he was being deceived. Indeed, he became convinced of it when Ysopete forcefully told him that death would be preferable to continuing on in the direction Turk was leading them. Quivira, Ysopete insisted, was toward the northeast, not the east or southeast. Questioning of Tejas Indians indicated that Turk, indeed, had been taking them away from their goal.

Coronado decided that the time had come to find out the truth. He summoned Turk and subjected him to a thorough grilling. Turk finally broke and admitted that he had been deceiving the Spaniards. Coronado demanded to know "why he had lied and had guided them so far out of their way," and Turk confessed that the people at Pecos Pueblo "had asked him to lead them off onto the plains and lose them, so that the horses would die when their provisions gave out, and they [the Spaniards] would be so weak if they ever returned that they could be killed without any trouble, and thus they could take revenge for what had been done to them."

As clever as he was, Turk had not become aware that horses, no less than buffalo and other grazing animals, would have thrived on the rich grass of the Great Plains. He had supposed that the Spaniards did not know how to live without certain types of food, and would not have been able to survive by hunting and eating the fare of plains Indians. He admitted, as well, that "as for gold, he did not know where there was any of it. He said this like one who had given up hope . . ." Coronado put him in chains, and appointed Ysopete chief guide.

Now Coronado drastically changed his plans. He

would go on to Quivira with a small party, and the army would be sent back to Tiguex on the Río Grande to await his return. "When the men in the army learned of this decision," said Castañeda, "they begged their general not to leave them to conduct the further search, but declared that they all wanted to die with him and did not want to go back."

But Coronado had made up his mind, and he rejected their pleas. Early in June, 1541, with thirty cavalrymen, six soldiers on foot, a priest, some extra horses, a pack-train, and several servants, he started north for Quivira. He had carefully selected the members of his company, taking only men whose mettle had been tested and whose loyalty was unquestionable. The disgraced and hopeless Turk was taken along in manacles. Coronado had not yet decided how to punish him.

From the Texas Panhandle their route crossed the Oklahoma Panhandle, west of the 100th Meridian, and went on to the plains of Kansas—all country never before entered by white men. They traveled slowly, making no more than eight to ten miles a day, holding to a course slightly northeast. Jaramillo wrote, "We continued on our way for . . . about thirty days of actual travel, although the marches were not long. We never lacked water in all these days, and we were always among the cattle, on some days seeing more of them than on others, depending upon the watering places we came to." Coronado differed with him about the water, when he wrote King Charles V: "We went without water for many days, and had to cook our food with cow dung, because there is no other fuel in all these plains . . ." He agreed with Jaramillo, however, that they were always among the buffalo, stating that on the journey they lived entirely on buffalo meat.

They reached the Arkansas River near the place where the town of Ford, Kansas, would stand several centuries later. Ysopete knew where he was, and said the villages of Quivira were not far to the northeast. No royal barge with a golden eagle on its prow appeared, as Turk had promised. There was nothing but plains, buffalo, and sky.

Yet Coronado continued to push on, refusing to abandon all hope. Something of value might still be discovered. He paused long enough to sit down beside the trail and address a letter to "The Governor of Harahey and Quivira," thinking that the ruler was "a Christian from the wrecked fleets of Florida." Jaramillo gave the only explanation as to why Coronado held such a conviction, stating that descriptions obtained from Indians of the government and society in Quivira "led us to entertain this opinion." How erroneous it was they would soon discover.

Crossing the great bend of the Arkansas River at the ford which had been used for countless centuries by Indians and buffalo, Coronado held to the northeast and reached the Smoky Hill River in the vicinity of Lindsborg, Kansas. There his trail ended.

Ysopete had told the truth. There were no large towns, no gold, no treasure of any kind . . . nothing except little villages occupied by Wichita Indians, half-

In Quivira, Coronado found, instead of gold, small villages inhabited by Wichita Indians.

naked, tattooed, and in appearance differing little from the Querechos and the Tejas.

Although Jaramillo thought the country beautiful and would be "productive of all sorts of commodities," one of his companions saw the scene in a somewhat less commendatory light, declaring the Quiviras were a "bestial people without any order in their dwellings or anything else." This severe critic of the Indians admitted only that Quivira was a better land than the New Mexico and Arizona deserts. At least, it contained great game herds, and there was not a shortage of water. Quivira might be an Indian paradise, but the Spaniards lived by other standards of value. The soldiers advocated that Turk be killed, but if Coronado was dispirited and hopeless, he was not bloodthirsty. He demurred in giving the order that would put an end to the miserable former guide who was still in chains.

He called a meeting of all his men and, as Jaramillo reported, "asked them what we ought to do, remembering that we had left the army behind and we were here. It seemed to everybody that, since it was almost the beginning of winter . . . and since there were so few of us . . . his Lordship ought to turn back . . ."

Meanwhile, the desperate Turk was making every effort to save his life. Ysopete, who had been loyal and honest throughout the long march, revealed that Turk was conniving with Indians to kill the horses. If this could be accomplished the Spaniards, few in number, would be on foot among hundreds of Indians, and could easily be wiped out.

Coronado, who once had demanded "What honor could be gained by killing the Indian?" now changed his mind. He ordered that Turk be executed. Contreras, Coronado's chief groom, carried the order to the· assigned executioners and stated that a "soldier named Pérez . . . from behind put a rope around the Turk's neck, twisted it with a garrote, and choked him to death."

The party started back to Tiguex, where the main force was waiting for them, and Wichita guides showed them a more direct route. They spent the winter in the pueblos on the Río Grande.

For Coronado and his soldiers the great dream had been destroyed by stark reality. They knew the truth—there were no great cities, no streets filled with silver workers, no streams flowing in beds of gold, no mountain of jewels. There were only deserts, snowcapped ranges, endless plains, and sky. In April, 1542, Coronado and his once powerful army, now tattered, weary, poorly equipped, and completely dispirited, left Tiguex on the long and sad march back to Mexico.

Not everyone who had come north with Coronado two years before had failed to find treasure. In the eyes of three padres and several religious lay brothers both the land of the Pueblo Indians and Quivira were among the richest countries on earth. They had found what to them was the greatest treasure of all—heathen souls to be saved. Coronado granted their request to remain and dedicate themselves to the service of God among the infidels.

Fray Luis de Escalona with one assistant, a Negro named Cristobal, chose to conduct his missionary work at Pecos Pueblo. Coronado gave him a few sheep. There, according to one historian, he lived in a poor little hut, more like a cave, "where the Indians ministered to him his meager sustenance, consisting of tortillas, beans, and a little atole." His fate is not known, for he was never seen again by white men.

Fray Juan de la Cruz, it is believed, remained at Tiguex. It was reported to later explorers that he was murdered by Indians who were opposed to "his teachings and the counsels by which he urged them to detest their barbarous customs."

Fray Juan de Padilla, known to Coronado's soldiers as "the fighting priest" because of his bravery in battle, returned to Quivira. With him he took as lay brothers a Portuguese, Andrés do Campo, and two Indians, Lucas and Sebastian, who had come with him from Mexico. Coronado supplied them with equipment, religious paraphernalia, and a small band of sheep.

More may be told of Fray Padilla than of the other martyrs. The Quiviras had welcomed him, and had willingly permitted him to establish a mission. After working among them for a few months, he decided to explore country farther to the east. The Quiviras advised him not to go, warning that he would encounter people who were their enemies.* But Fray Padilla was determined to make the journey, and with do Campo, Lucas and Se-

* The Quiviras may have been talking about Indians called Guas, who later would be known as Kansa, the tribe from which the name of the State of Kansas derived.

bastian he set out, their supplies and baggage carried on the only horse they possessed.

They had traveled no more than a few days when they saw approaching them a large number of warriors in full battle array. Fray Padilla seemed at once to sense that his end had come, and he commanded do Campo, Lucas and Sebastian to flee to safety on the horse. They obeyed, and then, according to an early Spanish document, Fray Padilla "fell on his knees, and, beginning to pray, he awaited the fury of the barbarians who were coming near, commending his soul to that Lord for whose love and faith he offered it. The cruel butchers in a twinkling filled him with arrows, and thus the unfortunate man died."

Lucas and Sebastian went back when the warriors had gone and buried Fray Padilla, then rejoined do Campo.

For nearly five years the Portuguese and the two Christian Indians wandered in the wilderness. Their ordeals and experiences in Kansas, Oklahoma, Texas and northern Mexico, comprise one of the most thrilling sagas of North American exploration. At last they reached the Mexican Province of Pánuco, which had been the goal of the ill-fated Narváez Expedition of which Cabeza de Vaca, Dorantes, Castillo and Estevanico the Black had been the only survivors.

In March, 1547, a high royal official in Mexico City reported to the Spanish Government: "Very great are the things told of by a Portuguese who escaped from a province where the Indians killed a friar, and who, not knowing where he was going, by the will of God was brought to this city, with such great news of the land and its people that everybody marvels."

The great dream was temporarily revived. Although do Campo and his companions described Quivira as a bountiful land containing great herds of game and many Indians, being honest men they made no claim that precious metals existed there. It did not matter. The people in Mexico City believed what they wanted to believe.

For a time rumors were circulated that Coronado had gone to the wrong places, or had not gone far enough, and a great new expedition was to be sent north to recover the fortunes he had missed. The talk was exciting, but nothing would come of it.

8 / THE FORGOTTEN LAND

For almost four decades after Coronado's return no official attention was given to the vast territory that he had crossed. No more dreaming, hopeful conquistadors followed the trails opened by Estevanico the Black, Fray Marcos, Alarcón, Tovar, Cárdenas, Melchior Díaz and others. Indeed, more was forgotten about the discoveries and feats of all these daring men than was remembered.

There were good reasons for this situation. Mexico had become in many respects a land of turmoil, and the provincial government had its hands full trying to keep order and enforce the royal decrees that came to it from Spain. Since the conquest of Cortez, in 1519, thousands of Spaniards had crossed the Atlantic Ocean to seek their fortune in the land he had conquered. Steadily the frontier had been pushed westward and northward from central Mexico. Mines were opened and ranches were established. Always with the vanguard of the pioneers, and often ahead of them, were missionaries, willing to sacrifice their lives in the work of converting the natives to Christianity. Missions and convents were built in the wilderness, and soldiers guarded them. Towns whose inhabitants showed little respect for any law grew whereever minerals and good grazing and farming lands were discovered. Although the Indians fought courageously in defense of their homes and fields, they were unable to counter the devastating and deadly fire from Spanish guns. Tribe after tribe was subdued as the adventurers drove on in a constant quest for new riches. In violation of Spanish laws uncounted thousands of Indians were enslaved and forced to work without pay for mine owners, cattlemen and ranchers and in other types of commercial enterprises.

By 1567 the wild conquest had been carried northward, into the region now known as Chihuahua, the vast Mexican State bordered today on the north by the American State of New Mexico. Fabulous strikes of silver, gold and other metals were made in this area, which the Spanish called Nueva Viscaya. The center of the rich mining region was Santa Bárbara, a town on the Florida River that rapidly became the most renowned place in northern Mexico. To it and the surrounding country swarmed adventurers, cattlemen, miners, farmers, priests and slave traders.

One result of this stampede was inevitable. Santa Bárbara was on the very edge of the Mexican frontier, and as the years passed both prosperous men and zealous padres began to think about pushing farther north. What, they wondered, was to be found there? New kingdoms to be conquered? More treasures of gold and silver? The only answers they received came out of their imaginations, out of their dreams. If they had ever known of the disastrous conquest of Coronado, which is doubtful, they had forgotten about it. In the latter half of the sixteenth century no histories were available to the residents of the remote frontier. Indeed, there were almost no printed books, except religious tracts, to be found in all of Mexico.

Thinking about solving the mysteries of the country to the north of Santa Bárbara was much easier than undertaking the task. In 1573 new legislation had been enacted to govern explorations and the establishment of settlements. Expeditions of discovery could be undertaken only by permission of the King, or at least by the Viceroy serving as his agent. Royal approval of explorations—they were to be called conquests no longer—would be given only to persons of good character, who had shown themselves to be devout Christians, and who could be depended upon to treat Indians with kindness and justice. The new code favored missionaries, and provided that any priests who were given official authority to engage in discoveries of new lands were to be provided with all necessities they required. Soldiers were to be assigned to protect them on their dangerous missions.

Fray Augustín Rodríguez was the first missionary to reopen the northern gateway which had remained closed since the heartbroken Coronado had put the Río Grande behind him, nearly forty years earlier.

For ten years Fray Augustín had lived among the

Conchos Indians of Chihuahua, and he had been eminently successful in enlisting them under the banners of Christianity. They had told him of other peoples who dwelt far to the north and who knew nothing of the word of God. For a long time he had dreamed of journeying to these idolatrous tribes, and awakening them to the blessings of salvation. At last, in 1580, he decided the time had come to take action. In compliance with the law, he went to Mexico City, seeking permission to go on the expedition. The plan he placed before the Viceroy, Don Lorenzo Suárez de Mendoza, Marquis de la Coruna, was approved.* A military escort, commanded by Captain Francisco Sánchez Chamuscado, was assigned to accompany him.

The rediscovery of the Southwest began, but it would be far from merely a repetition of the discoveries made four decades earlier. Actually, Coronado and his contemporaries had passed through a relatively small part of the vast region. There remained enormous areas no white man had explored, and some sections would remain unknown for another hundred years.

The purposes of the Rodríguez-Chamuscado Expedition were clearly set forth by Captain Chamuscado's aide, Hernán Gallegos, who wrote a narrative of the journey for the Viceroy. In addition to protecting the three missionaries who would go along, Chamuscado's duty, as the military head of the party, was to "carry out the discovery of New Mexico and the new lands—which

* Not the same Mendoza who was Viceroy in the time of Coronado.

had been sought for so many years." The major intention of the company, however, was to go "where God our Lord was pleased to direct them, in order that His Holy faith might be taught and His gospel spread throughout the lands which they . . . might thus discover in His holy service and in the interest of the royal crown."

They started from Santa Bárbara early in June, 1581. In the group, besides Fray Augustín, were two other padres, Francisco López and Juan de Santa María. The military contingent under Chamuscado consisted of only eight men. The Viceroy had authorized a force of twenty volunteers, but Chamuscado apparently had been unable to obtain that many. Gallegos stated that all who wished to go were required to pay their own expenses and furnish their arms and horses. Most soldiers of the ranks at frontier posts were poor, if not without any resources at all. Undoubtedly those who volunteered not only had the means of meeting the requirements but were convinced that the venture was worth any sacrifice they might make. If a gold or silver mine were discovered they would share in the profits.

Supplies, equipment, ammunition, and goods to be used in bartering with the Indians were carried on pack animals. Nineteen Indians had been engaged as servants and as wranglers for six hundred head of livestock and ninety horses. Animals were more easily obtained than soldiers, for every mission owned herds of cattle and sheep, and the cost of employing Indians was negligible, involving little more than the expense of feeding them.

From Santa Bárbara the company followed a well-worn trail down the Conchos River. This was country in which slave raids had been conducted, and it was with difficulty that Fray Augustín was able to convince the Indians that they came in peace and would not harm them. The people whom Gallegos called Conchas and Rayas were "unattractive in appearance. They go about naked like savages. They are lazy, capable of little work, and dirty, and sustain themselves on quantities of calabashes, ground mesquite, mescal, prickly pears, and fish from the river." *

A few days later they encountered another tribe, the Julimes, who were "very handsome, spirited, and much more active and intelligent than the people met previously. They are very well built. Their faces, arms, and bodies are striped with neatly painted lines. These people are cleaner and more modest than the Conchas." They, too, lived in terror of slavers. Many of them had run away and were hiding in the mountains. Fray Augustín planted crosses in their towns "so that in case any Spaniards did come with the intention of doing harm they would refrain, on seeing the crosses. The Indians were very much pleased by this . . . ."

The same conditions prevailed until the company had reached the Río Grande and ascended it for a considerable distance, when they passed beyond the region in which slave raids had been made. One question was up-

* The manuscript of the Gallegos account of the Chamuscado-Rodriguez Expedition is preserved in the Archives of the Indies in Seville, Spain. The quotations in this chapter are from a translation of it made by Drs. George P. Hammond and Agapito Rey, published by the University of New Mexico.

permost in Fray Augustín's thoughts, and he asked it of all Indians with whom they talked. He had been told by the converts at his mission that there were people who dwelt far to the north, wore cotton clothing, lived in large towns with buildings many stories high, were rich in corn and hides, but knew nothing of the Christian God. Were there such people?

Always the answer was *yes.* "In view of this we offered many thanks to God our Lord for the encouraging information . . . and for the news concerning the supplies of corn, which was the thing we most desired. As long as we did not lack corn and other food we would march on until we came to the end of the land and saw all that was to be discovered in it, especially the people with the fixed domiciles, among whom the holy gospel might be planted and taught . . ."

As they continued up the valley of the Río Grande "there was not a day or night when we were not accompanied by more than three hundred souls." One day, in an Indian town, Fray Augustín casually inquired if any other white men ever had passed that way. Everyone was startled by the reply. He was told that "a long time ago four Christians had passed through there."

They had heard about Cabeza de Vaca, Castillo, Dorantes and Estevanico the Black. Forty-five years had passed since the four strangers had appeared out of the rising sun and had gone on in search of the sea, but the memory of them was still vivid among the Jumanos of the Río Grande.

As they continued up the Río Grande to the site of El

Paso, they met more Indians who appeared to be well informed about people to the north "who lived in large houses three and four stories high, cultivated large areas of land, had fowls, and many cotton blankets which they wore, for they gathered large quantities of that crop, with bolls as big as one's fist, wore shoes, made pottery from which they ate . . ." The northern people were "numerous, very brave and warlike . . ."

The great pueblos were not far ahead, and the padres were eager and excited, and "nourished great hopes of emerging victorious . . ."

Regrettably, the Gallegos narrative contains few dates, and for this reason it can only be said that on a midsummer day in the year 1581 they entered the future State of New Mexico.

The first large pueblo they found was abandoned, but once had been "inhabited by a large number of people, who must have been very advanced, judging by the buildings, and whose discovery would be of great importance, if they could be found." The next day, after traveling two more leagues up the Río Grande, they reached a town "of many houses three stories high," but found no inhabitants. They had left the night before, "because they had noticed our approach. In the houses were found many turkeys and much cotton and corn . . . We did not dare to take any of the goods, for we wanted the people to know we did not intend to harm them. We found the houses very well planned and built in blocks, with mud walls, whitewashed inside and well decorated with monsters, other animals, and human figures . . .

The inhabitants have a great deal of crockery. . . . all decorated and of better quality than the pottery of New Spain."

They were now in the present Doña Ana County, New Mexico, and they were passing through country never before traversed by white men. That did not mean that the Indians, who were Piros, did not know that white men existed. From people farther north had come tales of the trail of blood Coronado's army had left on its march across northern New Mexico. But Fray Augustín was able to find some of the people who had fled from the pueblo and convince them that he and his company meant no harm, and the "news that we were coming in peace spread so widely that there was not a day when we were not surrounded and accompanied. . . . They indicated to us that there were in their nation twenty-odd pueblos, and that farther on was another nation, with which they were at war. . . . we continued up the river."

Upon reaching the Galisteo Valley, only twenty miles southwest of the site on which the New Mexican capital of Santa Fe would be built three decades later, they camped at a large pueblo that they called Malpartida. The area was rough and mountainous, and "we asked if there were many minerals in the region, showing the natives the samples we had taken along. . . . and requesting them to lead us to the place where such riches might be found. They immediately brought us a large quantity of different kinds, including some of a coppery steellike ore. This mineral appeared to be rich. . . . they gave us to understand that there were many minerals near the province. . . . We went to investigate and discovered mines of different ores."

Treasure and countless souls to be saved . . . Both the soldiers and the friars were happy. They asked what lay ahead. Said the inhabitants of Malpartida: More pueblos to the north and west, and to the east, not far distant, great plains on which millions of buffalo grazed.

". . . we decided to find the herds and to explore the land in which they lived. . . . The region must be fertile and have many grassy plains and plenty of water, to judge by the number of buffalo the natives said there were. Taking up some handfuls of soil, they said that the animals were just as numerous as the grains of sand in their hands. . . ." Such a bountiful country certainly was worth investigating.

Fray Juan de Santa María, however, had other ideas. He had decided to go home "to report of what had been discovered to his prelate and to his Excellency, the viceroy." Everyone was astounded and "condemned the decision as inadvisable, for he would not only endanger his own life, but imperil the soldiers, and in addition would jeopardize further exploration of the land. We urged him to wait until we had inspected everything about which the natives had informed us, and had gone to see the buffalo, in order that a complete report of all this might be taken. . . . as any account he could give now would be incomplete, since we had not seen the most important things." Fray Juan de Santa María would not listen to the arguments. On a September day he started back along the trail to Mexico—alone.

Saddened by his precipitous departure, the company,

guided by Indians, left for the buffalo plains. They were gone approximately a month, presumably traveling as far northeast as an unidentifiable branch of the Canadian River. They killed many buffalo and lived sumptuously on the good meat. Gallegos recorded that it was October 19 when they started on the return trip to the Galisteo Valley.

There the group learned that Fray Juan de Santa María had gone only a short distance on his homeward journey when he was ambushed and slain. Inquiries revealed that the Indians believed Fray Juan de Santa María "was going to bring more Christians in order to put them out of their homes." To prevent this, they "followed the friar and killed him after two or three days of travel."

Now it was learned—by what means Gallegos does not say—that the Indians were plotting to attack the entire company. "Seeing that they had killed the friar so easily, they thought they would kill us just as readily. From then on they knew we were mortal; up to that time they had thought us immortal." It was planned to "withdraw gradually" from the country, and to make every effort to avoid a fight. Nine armed men would have had little hope of halting an assault by several hundred warriors.

While they were camped near Malpartida, three horses were stolen and slaughtered by Indians from Malagón, an adjacent pueblo. Captain Chamuscado decided that in spite of their dangerous situation a show of strength had to be made. He sent five mounted men to Malagón to capture the culprits, "either peaceably or by

According to pre-arranged plan, the two Indian captives were rescued by Fray Augustín and Fray Francisco.

force." The soldiers demonstrated their bravery by riding boldly up to the gates of Malagón, a large town "of eighty houses of three and four stories with plazas and streets." Many of the inhabitants were gathered on the roofs, prepared to defend their homes.

When their demand that the horse thieves be surrendered was ignored, the soldiers opened fire, "although we incurred great risk in doing so, for we were only five men facing the task of attacking eighty houses with more than a thousand inhabitants." Terrified by the flame and roar of the harquebuses, the Indians left the rooftops and concealed themselves in the buildings.

Searching about, the soldiers found remains of the slaughtered horses. Another fusillade of shots ripped into the adobe walls. Several Indians ran out and attempted to escape. Two soldiers pursued them, and each seized one by the hair. Although "the natives were swift, the horses soon overtook them." The captives were taken back to Malpartida, and Chamuscado announced that they would be put to death.

This was a ruse, intended only to frighten the Indians. Chamuscado and the friars had agreed that just as the executions were about to be carried out, Fray Augustín and Fray Francisco would intervene and save the victims. This would make a good impression on the Indians, and inspire them to respect and fear the powers of the priests, both of whom were planning to remain in the country and establish a mission.

Preparations were begun, and Chamuscado ordered the soldiers "to place a block in the middle of the camp's plaza, where the rest of the Indians were watching, and to cut off the heads of the prisoners. . . . All was so done. At the moment when the soldiers were about to cut off the heads of the Indians, the friars came out in flowing robes and saved the captives from their perilous plight. As we pretended that we were going to seize them, the Indians who were watching immediately took hold of the friars and the prisoners and carried all of them off to their houses, mindful of the great support they had found in the priests. Because of what we had done and proposed to do, the natives became so terrified of us that it was surprising how they trembled. . . . The following morning, many Indians from the pueblo of Malagón came, heavily laden with turkeys and other foods for our use, entreating us not to be angry with them. . . ." The company marched on north, narrowly escaping a perilous situation.

They saw the great town on the Pecos and visited the numerous pueblos in the valley of the Río Grande between the present Santa Fe and Albuquerque. They were on Coronado's trail now. Going on west they passed Acoma, the Sky City, and reached the pueblos of Zuñi. Here they were told of the Hopi Towns, which Cárdenas and Tovar had visited in 1540, and they learned that only a few days ahead was a large mineral deposit, but they did not go to find the ore "because we had not brought the necessary provisions."

At Zuñi Captain Chamuscado and his soldiers "decided to return to the land of Christians"—Mexico—"before any misfortune should befall them. . . ." It was December, 1581, and the snow was deep.

Traveling slowly over the high, cold country of northern New Mexico they reached the pueblo of Puaray sometime in January, 1582. It was this town which the friars had selected as the site of their mission, where they would remain and carry on their religious work of converting the Indians to Christianity.

The exact location of Puaray is still a matter of dispute among archeologists. A large pueblo, containing "one hundred and twenty-four houses two and three stories high," it stood on the Río Grande somewhere between Albuquerque and Bernalillo. Some authorities think it was a part of Tiguex, where Coronado and his men fought the fiercest and bloodiest battle of their long journey and where they spent two miserable winters. Puaray, however, was destroyed long before the era of scientific investigation, and the many ruins in the vicinity have defeated archeologists in their efforts to identify its site with indisputable evidence.

When the two padres informed Chamuscado of their decision to remain in Puaray, he pleaded fervently with them "in the name of God and of his Majesty, to leave with us. . . . for they would be in great danger. He added that they could not accomplish any good results at present, before there were Spanish forces to compel the natives to obey their wishes." In spite of Chamuscado's "exhortations and those of the soldiers in this matter, the friars replied that they were determined to remain, that no one could force them to abandon their pious intention of preaching the holy gospel, and that they would excommunicate any person who attempted to thwart them."

On the last day of January, 1582, Fray Augustín Rodríguez and Fray Francisco López stood in their tattered robes before the gate of Puaray, made the sign of the Cross, and waved goodbye to their companions with whom they had shared so many adventures and made so many noteworthy discoveries.

The little homeward-bound company followed the trail down the Río Grande. They had traveled "more than eighty leagues"—which would place them in southern New Mexico—"when God willed that Captain Chamuscado should be stricken with an old ailment." Several other soldiers soon became ill, and they frequently were forced to stop for several days until the stricken found the strength to continue. "Because the captain was a man of sixty or seventy years, the ailment took firmer hold on him than on the others who were not so old. . . . Since his condition was caused by exhaustion, we decided to bleed him. As the equipment ". . . had been left with the friars, we proceeded as soldiers do in time of need when they draw blood with a horseshoe nail and apply the medicines by means of a horn."

Chamuscado commended himself to God and made his last will before Gallegos, who was a notary. His affliction "was becoming so serious that his hands and feet were paralyzed, and therefore we decided to build a litter which, slung between two horses, could take him quickly to Christian lands where the holy sacraments could be administered. . . . Burdened by this device, we traveled with great difficulty."

They were within thirty leagues of Santa Bárbara when Captain Chamuscado died. He was given "the best burial possible. . . . God knows the depression, grief, and pity that we all experienced at seeing him die in such a remote and desolate land, without spiritual or temporal comfort."

On Easter Sunday, April 15, 1582, the residents of Santa Bárbara were startled by the sound of guns being fired at the edge of town. Peering cautiously out of their houses they saw a ragged group of horsemen and Indians approaching, and, as Gallegos recorded, "we were given an especially warm welcome because the inhabitants had thought us dead."

Couriers were soon riding fast toward Mexico City with news of the expedition's return. Once again tales spread like an epidemic of fever. Fabulous mines had been discovered. Gallegos had presented the Viceroy with incredibly rich samples of ore. Fray Augustín and the dead Captain Chamuscado had taken possession in the name of the King of a vast unknown territory that contained not only fabulous mines but endless pastures, rich valleys, immense forests, and—most important of all, of course—great numbers of heathen Indians who were eager to become Christians.

A handful of soldiers, at their own expense, had succeeded where Coronado, with an army, had failed, and their success "brought great relief and inspiration to many people in New Spain."

Among those who were especially fascinated by the reports of Gallegos and the other soldiers were the mine owners, cattlemen, military officers, government officials and bold adventurers of the frontier Province of Nueva Viscaya and the rapidly growing, unruly city of Santa Bárbara. As if held by a magnet, their eyes were fastened on the north, and they saw there visions that made their hearts race and set fires in their blood.

9 / THE RESCUE

Antonio de Espejo was a daring young adventurer who had arrived in Mexico from Spain in 1571. He was then serving as a confidential officer of the Inquisition, but he was driven by an ambition to make a much greater fortune than was possible in the work of exposing heretics or officials disloyal to the Church.

Espejo was intelligent, shrewd and tough, but he was not crude, and he could be persuasive, diplomatic and charming. While continuing to hold his post as a spy for the Inquisition, he entered into the cattle trade and soon acquired the means to live in refinement and comfort. Bold and quick-tempered, he was not fearful of taking the law into his own hands to protect his rights and property. When a number of his cattle were stolen, he and two of his vaqueros (cowboys) traced them to a stockyard and recovered them at gunpoint.

Although he maintained his political and church affili-ations in Mexico City, Espejo, like so many other adventurers, was attracted by the opportunities on the northern frontier. He and his brother, Pedro, soon became successful cattle ranchers.

On more than one occasion the Espejo brothers demonstrated that they were equal to the wild and rugged life of the country. Antonio killed an Indian cowboy, and they were involved in numerous violent encounters in which blood was shed. During a roundup in the spring of 1581, several vaqueros deserted after Antonio had threatened their lives. A gunfight followed in a nearby town, and Pedro killed one of the deserters and wounded another. Both Espejos were charged with murder and taken to Mexico City. Pedro was sentenced to prison, but Antonio was fined. Instead of paying, he fled to Chihuahua. If anyone there knew he was a wanted man, no one seemed to care.

Espejo was in Santa Bárbara, or nearby, when the soldiers of Captain Chamuscado returned with their wondrous tales. He quickly recognized what he thought was an opportunity to get rich, or richer, by finding the mines which the soldiers said existed in the Río Grande country. Understanding that the Franciscans were deeply concerned about the welfare of the priests who had been left at Puaray, Espejo shrewdly announced his willingness to lead an expedition to rescue them.

Government officials, anxious to participate and reap the rewards, recommended that a large company be sent. This could not be done without authorization from the Viceroy and perhaps from the King. Efforts were made to obtain a permit, but red tape and delay were encountered in Mexico City. The Franciscans became impatient, and they readily accepted Espejo's offer to pay the expenses of a small rescue party. Fray Bernardino Beltrán, who would go along, offered to obtain the necessary permit. There is some doubt as to who actually issued it. One account states that the authority was obtained by Fray Beltrán from his superior, but another document relates that it was granted by the lieutenant-governor of Nueva Viscaya. Whatever the truth, the expedition was organized, and Espejo paid most of the bills.

Espejo enlisted fourteen soldiers to accompany the party. One of them, Miguel Sánchez Valenciano, took along his wife and three small sons, the youngest only twenty months old. Although Espejo prepared a report of the journey, the best account of it was written by one of the soldiers, Diego Pérez de Luxán.* Several Indians were engaged as servants, to care for the packtrain carrying provisions, arms and equipment, and to tend a herd of one hundred and fifteen horses. Several friars had planned to make the journey, but Fray Beltrán was finally the only one to go.

The little company left the Valle de Allende, a short distance east of Santa Bárbara, on November 10, 1582. There were good reasons for starting so late in the year to travel to a high cold country in which they could expect to find deep snow. On the part of Fray Beltrán it was

---

* Espejo's report was first printed in Spain in 1586. It and Luxán's account of the Espejo Expedition have appeared in numerous histories. The quotations in this chapter are from translations made by Drs. George P. Hammond and Agapito Rey, published by the University of New Mexico.

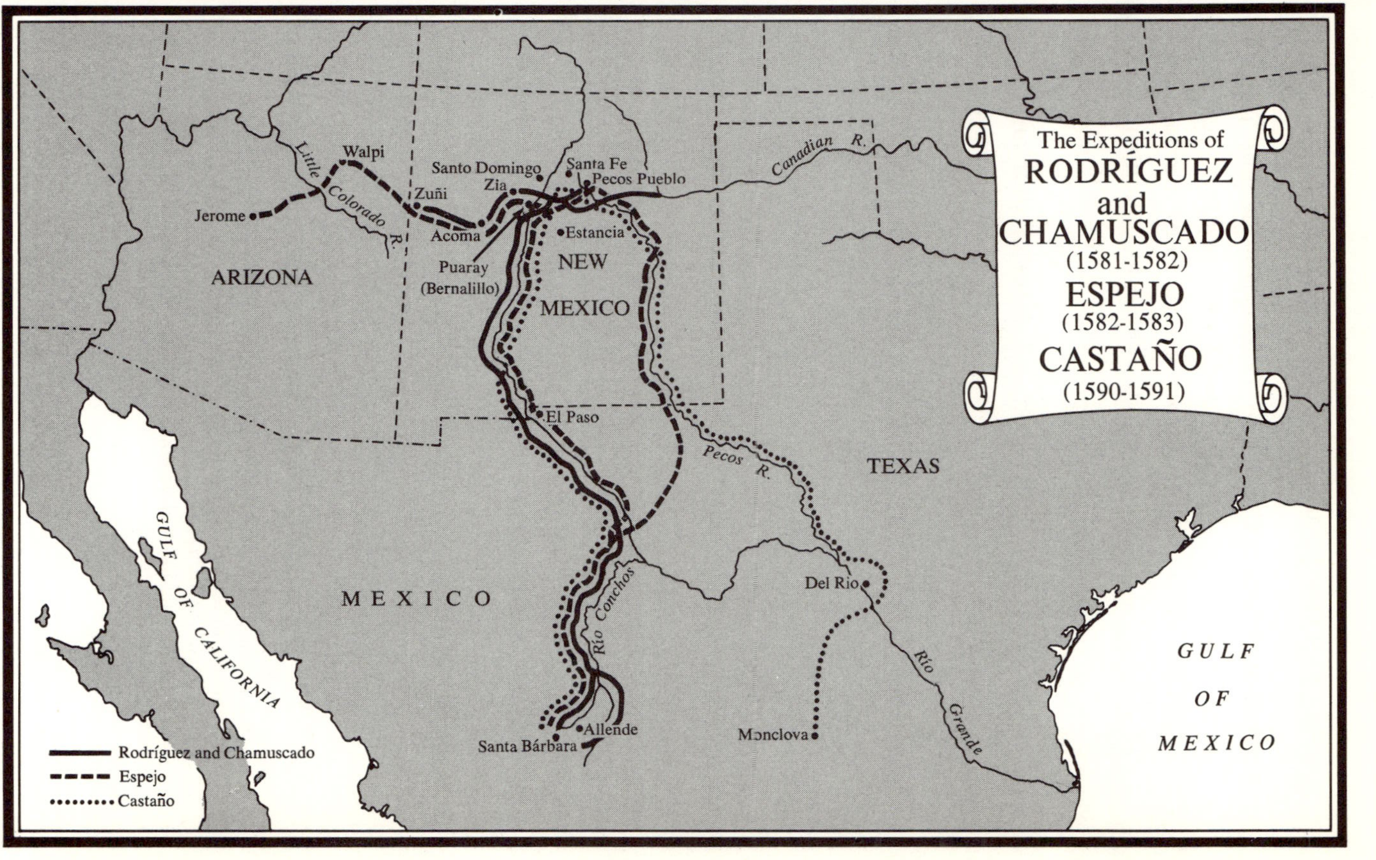

The Expeditions of
RODRÍGUEZ and CHAMUSCADO
(1581-1582)
ESPEJO
(1582-1583)
CASTAÑO
(1590-1591)
ARIZONA
NEW MEXICO
TEXAS
MEXICO
GULF OF CALIFORNIA
GULF OF MEXICO
Little Colorado R.
Colorado R.
Canadian R.
Pecos R.
Rio Conchos
Rio Grande
Jerome
Walpi
Zuñi
Santo Domingo
Zia
Acoma
Puaray (Bernalillo)
Santa Fe
Pecos Pueblo
Estancia
El Paso
Del Rio
Monclova
Santa Bárbara
Allende
Rodríguez and Chamuscado
Espejo
Castaño

eagerness to learn the fate of the padres who had remained at Puaray. A former servant of the dead Captain Chamuscado had picked up a report from Conchos Indians that the friars had been slain and that the Puaray country was in revolt. Fray Beltrán left, praying that the report was not true, but there was only one way to find out. On the part of Espejo, it was to locate mines, take possession of them and be hailed as the conqueror of the country. He was well aware that if he delayed in the attempt he would find himself facing stiff competition, for many wealthy persons in Mexico, as well as the highest officials, were planning conquests.

The expedition followed the customary trail down the Conchos River and turned northward in the Valley of the Río Grande. Here they, too, met Indians who told them of Cabeza de Vaca, and "men, women and children came to have the sign of the cross made over them." The stories of the God in Heaven which Cabeza de Vaca had told them had been preserved through the years, handed down from very old men who had heard them, and they had lost none of their drama and meaning. The children knew them well.

At a pueblo on the Río Grande, they met an Indian whom they called Juan Cantor. He had served as an interpreter with the Rodríguez-Chamuscado Expedition. Juan Cantor, who could speak Spanish, stated he had learned from various Indians "that the report that the friars [who had stayed at Puaray] were dead was false; that on the contrary they were alive, that the Conchos Indians who had brought the news [that they were dead] had fled, having made the statement in fear of punishment." Greatly cheered by the news, Fray Beltrán urged that they press ahead with all possible speed, and the company moved on up the Río Grande.

At the beginning of February, 1583, they passed the site of the present Elephant Butte Dam, and about a week later reached two pueblos.* Here they were told again that Fray Augustín Rodríguez and Fray Francisco López had been murdered, and that the people of Puaray and other Tiguex pueblos were on the warpath.

Luxán recorded that there was "a great deal of discussion." The majority of the soldiers wanted to abandon the quest and go home, but some "suggested that we should seek a convenient place in which to build a fortress where the camp might remain with seven soldiers while the other eight went on" to make certain "whether the friars were dead or alive." Espejo and two or three men were strongly opposed to dividing the small force, and their arguments finally prevailed.

The company learned the sad truth about ten days later when they reached Tiguex. The people of Puaray and the other adjacent towns had fled to the mountains, "because all had taken part in killing the friars, and the servants who had remained with them."

The Spaniards tried to induce the people to return, assuring the Indians that they had no intention of punishing them, "but they refused." In the next few days "we inspected some pueblos. All were deserted, but con-

* Near Socorro, New Mexico.

*Friendly Indians from distant pueblos presented Espejo
with turkeys and urged him to visit their towns.*

tained large quantities of corn, beans, green and sun-dried calabashes, and other vegetables; also dew-lapped cocks and hens, and a lot of pottery. We provisioned our-selves well with these things."

Word of the presence of the Spaniards had been car-ried throughout the country, and "Indians came from eight or ten leagues up the river with presents of tur-keys, telling us they were friendly and begging us to go to their pueblos, where they would serve us."

Once more some of the soldiers advocated turning homeward, inasmuch as it had been established that the two padres had been martyred. Espejo coldly rejected the proposal. Rescuing the friars had been only one pur-pose of the expedition. Friendly Indians had told of other "rich provinces," both to the east and to the west. Their tales excited him. Who knew what treasures might be discovered? In some of the deserted towns of Tiguex, Espejo had found "many ores of different col-ors"—evidence enough to convince him that his dream of finding minerals had a very good chance of being ful-filled.

Turning back at this point was unthinkable, but he glossed over his private emotions with the tactful state-ment that "this was a good opportunity for me to serve his Majesty by visiting and exploring the lands so new and so remote, with a view to informing his Majesty about them while incurring no expense to him for their exploration. Consequently, I decided to press forward as long as my strength permitted. . . . we continued our expedition and explorations in the same way as hereto-fore."

The reports of Luxán and Espejo are in large parts unclear and confusing. In both, the chronology frequently is incorrect, with the result that in many respects the itinerary remains obscure. If, however, it may not always be stated where they were at a specified time, there can be no doubt as to the extent of their travels. Moreover, it may be justifiably stated that they completed a journey that ranks among the most daring, comprehensive, and informative in the history of southwestern exploration.

Before reaching Puaray they made a side trip east of the Manzano Mountains, in the area where Fray Juan de Santa María had been murdered as he was on his way back to Mexico. From Puaray they set out westward, passing Zia, and Acoma. Although both the Coronado and Rodríguez-Chamuscado Expeditions had passed twice through this country, Espejo's company was the first to have met the Navajos. The encounter occurred at a pueblo not far from Acoma, when a band of Navajos came down from the high country in the vicinity of Mount Taylor to trade "salt, game (such as deer, rabbits, and hares), dressed chamois skins, and other goods in exchange for cotton blankets and various articles accepted in payment." Espejo was informed that in the country of the Navajo "mountain dwellers" mines and other riches were to be found, "but we did not go to inspect them because the natives there were numerous and warlike."

Well supplied with provisions, they went on, passing El Morro (the famous Inscription Rock on which many later explorers would carve their names), and late in March arrived at Zuñi. They were now at the westernmost point reached by the Rodríguez-Chamuscado party.

Here again there was dissention. The Zuñis informed Espejo about the towns of the Hopis which were far to the west, and intimated that mines were to be found in that direction. The Zuñis warned, however, that the Hopis were unfriendly and would attack the Spaniards. Espejo was determined to go on. A number of others were as determined to remain, declaring they had gone far enough and the mission undertaken had been completed. There was, wrote Luxán, "much controversy," which ended with Espejo and nine soldiers setting out for the Hopi Towns, and Fray Beltrán and the others remaining in Zuñi. Fortunately, Luxán, the diarist, elected to stay with Espejo and keep an account of the journey.

It was the middle of April, 1583, when Espejo left Zuñi. Eighty Zuñi warriors, obviously spoiling for a fight, volunteered to accompany him, stating that they wanted to "help us against the Mojose [Hopis]." Among them were two "Mexican Christian Indian brothers, Andrés and Gaspar, who had been left there by Coronado." The brothers must have been middle-aged, for forty years had passed since the last of Coronado's army departed from Zuñi. Luxán thought the volunteers were "influenced by Andrés and Gaspar," and "showed a fine spirit, saying they wanted to die wherever the Spaniards died. . . . we cut up pieces of red felt and put a colored sign on each man's head so that all could be recognized, and determined to attack unless the enemy submitted peacefully at once."

Information obtained from Indians along the trail

that the Hopis were prepared to attack the invaders proved to be false. Indeed, the opposite was true. The Hopis deluged both Spaniards and Zuñis "with tortillas, tamales, roasted green-corn ears, corn and other things. . . . asked for peace, and with trembling said it was a rumor falsely raised against them that they wanted to make war on us."

So it was that "the Lord willed that the whole land should tremble for ten lone Spaniards, when there were over twelve thousand Indians in the province, armed with bows and arrows. . . ." This, of course, was a gross exaggeration. If there had been twelve thousand Hopis present who were determined to launch an attack, no Spaniard would have survived to tell about it.

During several days of feasting and festivities in various Hopi pueblos it was learned that "riches of gold" were to be found a great distance to the southwest. Espejo consulted with his companions, and it was decided that, with Hopis guiding them, he and four soldiers should go in search of the mines. The others would return to Zuñi with the company's baggage, equipment and horses.

Espejo's boldness and courage was never better illustrated than on April 30, 1583, when he left Hopiland. With only four soldiers, men equally as brave as he, and several Hopi guides, he set off toward the southwest in the face of information that "the mines were far away, that there was a scarcity of water, and that the route was over difficult ridges."

Now Espejo was a true discoverer, as he and his little

band traveled through country never explored by white men. They crossed the Little Colorado River where the town of Winslow, Arizona, stands today, and turning more toward the west, passed places bearing the modern names of Salt Creek Canyon, Chavez Pass Canyon, Jay Cox Tank, Hay Lake, Cow Lake, Beaver Creek, and Montezuma's Castle. It was a magnificent, rugged land, crisscrossed by gorges and immense ridges that swept against the blue spring sky.

If the Indians along the trail had never seen Spaniards, they appeared to know much about them and what they were seeking. When they were in the vicinity of the Verde River, Luxán notes that "many mountain people waited for us with crosses painted on their heads, even the children. . . . They gave us ores as a sign of peace and many came to show us the mines. . . . we found many peaceful mountain people who received us well."

Near a peak called Black Mountain, a few miles west of the Verde River, they came to the end of their journey—the mines. A profoundly disappointed Luxán wrote that they were "so worthless that we did not find in any of them a trace of silver, as they were copper . . . and poor. We therefore determined to return at once." He would never know how wrong he was. Espejo and his men had found the great mines near Jerome, Arizona, from which Americans would later take vast fortunes in copper and silver.

In sharp contrast to Luxán's account was Espejo's report, which said: "I found the mines and took from them with my own hands ores which, according to experts on the matter, are very rich and contain a great deal of silver. . . . The general aspect of the land where the mines are located is good; there are rivers, marshes, woods, and also—on the riverbanks—great quantities of Castile grapes, walnut trees, flax, mulberries, maguey plants, and prickly pears. . . . The Indians in that land plant cornfields and have good houses."

The route they followed in returning to Zuñi remains in doubt, for once more the accounts of Luxán and Espejo differ. Espejo recorded that from the mines "we turned back. . . . the distance to Zuñi . . . being about seventy leagues. We wanted to return by a different way so as to have a better opportunity for observing and appraising the characteristics of the land, and I found a route more level than the one followed in going to the mines." He added that at Zuñi they found the soldiers from whom they had parted in the Hopi Towns, and also Fray Beltrán and the men who had remained with him. The Indians of Zuñi "had provided all of them with the food they needed. We all rejoiced greatly on being together again."

Luxán states that they left the mines on May 9, 1583, and returned to Zuñi by way of some Hopi pueblos, adding that "we traveled very fast and reached Sibola [Zuñi] on the seventeenth of the month. Here we found our companions in good health and well treated by these people, who were loyal and faithful."

Fray Beltrán and the men who had remained with him at Zuñi had suffered no ordeals nor faced any dangers, but they were far from happy, and they were more than ever determined to go directly back to Mexico over the shortest route. Espejo was equally as determined to continue his search for more mines in other areas and to return home by way of the buffalo plains. Luxán described the violent argument which took place. "To this proposal, Fray Beltrán (may God forgive him) and those who followed his views . . . replied that they were not willing to look for mines, but would return to the land of peace."

A soldier named Hernández "told everybody it was possible to escape from the land alive, and in this manner he was trying to promote his own interests and sow dissension among all. Hence he rebelled and raised the flag, demanding that the captain and the other comrades follow the king's standard."

Espejo took action, ordering Hernández "under penalty of death, loss of property, and conviction of treason, to continue the discovery of the land. . . . Since he would not desist but insisted on leaving, the flag was taken away from him by force."

Espejo refrained from arresting or punishing Hernández, however, "because we were so few, and also because we did not wish to cause disturbances among the natives." Espejo told Fray Beltrán that he was welcome to depart and take with him any men who wished to go, and with the padre went Hernández, Miguel Sánchez Valenciano and his family, and four other soldiers.

They started their homeward journey near the end of May, but no account of their experiences en route is known to have been written. Presumably they followed the trail down the Río Grande and up the Conchos River and its branches to Santa Bárbara. Whatever the case, sometime in the summer of 1583 they reached home in safety.

Espejo, the eight soldiers who had remained loyal to him (Luxán was one of them) and their servants and wranglers left Zuñi on the last day of May. They encountered trouble almost at once. Indians who had been friendly a few months earlier now fled from their path or closed their pueblos and refused to supply them with provisions. As they pushed eastward "so much news was brought to us to the effect that all the provinces were waiting to kill us, that it would have frightened any group of persons, even if they had been many, and the more so nine soldier companions, some poorly equipped. But trusting in God we marched steadily. . . ."

At Acoma, the Sky City, which they passed late in June, they "found the people of the pueblo in rebellion." Indians, among them Navajos, "kept shouting at us from the hills night and day. . . ." Several of the servants who had come with them from Mexico deserted out of fear. Although a search was made for them, only one was found, and he was mortally wounded.

They decided to give the "impudent Indians a surprise." As the soldiers prepared for an early morning attack, "they surprised us." Arrows suddenly rained on the Spaniards. They retaliated by setting fire to the Indians' homes and destroying "a very fine field of corn."

In another skirmish a few days later one soldier suffered arrow wounds in "the right cheek and right arm." By the time they reached Tiguex on the Río Grande, several others had been hurt or wounded and a number were sick. "Efforts were made to have the Indians come peacefully to us. . . . Instead, they remained in the hills and mocked us."

At Puaray, where the two friars had been murdered, Espejo's patience reached an end. Except for some thirty persons on the roof, the inhabitants of Puaray had fled. "When we asked them for food . . . they mocked us like the others." Espejo dispersed his little band and attacked. While four soldiers gained control of the "corners of the pueblo, four others with two servants began to seize those natives who showed themselves. We put them in an *estufa* [underground meeting place]. And as the pueblo was large and the majority had hidden themselves there, we set fire to it. . . . we thought some burned to death because of the cries they uttered.

"We at once took out the prisoners, two at a time, and lined them up against some cottonwoods . . . where they were garroted and shot many times until they were dead. Sixteen were executed, not counting those who burned to death.

"This was a remarkable deed for so few people in the midst of so many enemies."

The company went on, finding most of the people friendly, for "news of what had happened at Puaray spread through the provinces and the people were very much afraid and all served and regaled us."

From the Río Grande they struck eastward through the Galisteo Basin and reached the Pecos River. At the great Pecos Pueblo, where Coronado's advance guard had been so lavishly entertained, Espejo's requests for food were coldly refused. "Thereupon, six armed men entered the pueblo, determined to burn it, and the people were so frightened that they gave us the food against their will."

On the fifth day of July, 1583, they left Pecos Pueblo "and took two Indians by force to direct us to the buffalo." As they followed the Pecos River southward they were once more entering country that was totally unknown to white men.

Again notable discrepancies appear in the accounts of Luxán and Espejo. Luxán's report states: "The land is all very level, containing fine pastures and many water holes. . . . we found many buffalo tracks as well as bones and skulls. . . . In all this trip we did not find any buffalo, nothing but many tracks." They were, he said, "greatly troubled by lack of food," and thought fish caught in the river "quite a treat." Espejo's narrative, much briefer and less detailed, stated "we saw great numbers of the native cattle."

As far as can be determined, the company remained close to the Pecos River for several hundred miles until they came to the vicinity of Toyah Lake, in western Texas. On the seventh or eighth of August they met three Jumano Indians who told them that if they continued to follow the Pecos they would be going far out of their way. The Jumanos offered "to take us by good trails [directly] to the Río Grande. . . . This brought us no little joy."

They reached the Río Grande on August 16, and all

the Indians there "gave us a great reception . . . and presented us with quantities of ears of green corn, cooked and raw calabashes, and catfish. They put on great dances and festivities. . . . Our feeling of security was so great that we went about almost in shirt sleeves."

They were on a familiar trail now—up the Conchos and Florida Rivers. On September 10, 1583, having been gone approximately ten months, they rode into Allende, their starting place.

10 / TRAGIC JOURNEY

The machinery of the Spanish Government often was stalled by aggravating breakdowns, caused not so much by political dissension, religious controversies or the negligence of officials as by slow and unreliable communications. Under the most favorable conditions it took from four to six months for a dispatch to reach Mexico City from Seville. Not infrequently ships were lost at sea, and the royal mail sank with them. Reports from the Viceroy of New Spain to the King took the same time, or suffered the same disasters.

A similar situation prevailed in Mexico. It was fifteen hundred miles from the capital to the northern frontier. Mail had to be carried by horseback on tortuous trails that wound over great mountains and through deep canyons, thick forests, and badlands. Couriers met death by accident and at the hands of robbers and Indians, or sometimes simply vanished in the wilderness and were never found.

The discoveries of the Rodríguez-Chamuscado Expedition had confirmed the stories which had been kept in circulation by the Indians since the time of Coronado. Official reports left no doubt that an immense and bountiful land far north of Mexico contained a large number of people who lived in great houses. Even before Espejo had returned with more wonderful tales to tell, King Philip had revealed his interest in taking steps to establish a permanent colony in the undeveloped country. He thought the best method of procedure might be to contract with some responsible person to undertake the conquest, a man who could be depended upon to obey the laws controlling colonization, and who was qualified to serve as the first governor of the new Province of New Mexico.*

Fully aware that such a major project would be very expensive, would require thorough and efficient organization, and would be beset with legal and political complications, Mexican officials moved with thoughtful deliberation and extreme caution. Correspondence on the matter between government and religious officials, in both New Spain and Old Spain, assumed voluminous proportions. The slowness and difficulties of communications caused unavoidable delays, and years passed without a final decision being made.

Meanwhile, Espejo's glowing reports, which he had prepared in the fall of 1583, began to reach official ears in 1584. Before that, however, the ambitious men who

---

* The province would contain the entire Southwest of the future United States.

dominated affairs on the northern frontier knew their content.

In an account sent to the King, Espejo wrote of New Mexico:

"The natives of all those provinces are large, more vigorous than the Mexicans, and healthy, for no illness was noted among them. Their women are fairer than the Mexican women, and they are an intelligent and orderly people. There are attractive pueblos with plazas, and well-arranged houses. This indicates that the inhabitants would learn quickly any matter dealing with good government.

"In the greater part of those provinces, there is an abundance of game beasts and birds: rabbits, hares, deer, buffalo, ducks, geese, cranes, and pheasants and other birds. There are also fine wooded mountains with trees of all kinds, salines, and rivers containing a great variety of fish.

"Carts and wagons can be driven through most of this region; and there are good pastures for cattle as well as lands suitable for vegetables or grain crops, whether irrigated or depending on seasonal rains.

"There are many rich mines, too, from which I brought ores to be assayed and to determine their quality.

"I brought also an Indian man . . . and an Indian woman . . . so that they might enlighten us regarding those provinces and the road to that region, if its discovery and colonization are undertaken anew in the service of his Majesty, my intention being that these two Indians should learn the Mexican language and other tongues with this aim in view."

When it became known throughout Mexico that the King had proposed that New Mexico be colonized, a feverish competition ensued among prominent men who wanted to command the expedition and enjoy the honors and rewards they were convinced it would bring. Wealthy cattlemen, mine owners, political and military officials of northern Mexican States, and greedy adventurers made appeals for the appointment but to no avail. The wall of indecision in Mexico City remained intact.

In 1590 a new Viceroy of Mexico took office. He was Luis de Velasco, a son of a former Viceroy. With a new ruler in the Mexico City palace, the conquistadors hopeful of being turned loose to conquer New Mexico logically could reason that the delays would continue. Being unfamiliar with the problem, Velasco hardly could be expected to accept blindly the plans of his predecessor or to make a hasty decision of his own.

One veteran frontiersman, Gaspar Castaño de Sosa, determined that he would wait no longer. Castaño had been a pioneer settler in the northern Mexican Province of Nuevo León. He had been the first alcalde-mayor of Monterrey, and later lieutenant governor of the Province. Aggressive, energetic and unscrupulous, he had engaged in the Indian slave trade, had acquired mines and property, and had founded several settlements. He was far from being a poor man (selling captured Indians to ranchers and mine owners throughout the northern provinces had been profitable), but neither was he as rich as he had expected to be. His own mines had yielded little silver, and his hope of developing Nuevo León into a flourishing colony had not materialized.

*Castaño unscrupulously lured the people of Monclova
to join his expedition by showing them silver ore.*

Inspired to new dreams of achieving success by the reports of the Rodríguez-Chamuscado and the Espejo Expeditions, Castaño had twice sent emissaries to Mexico City to secure for him a license to conquer and settle the land of the Pueblos. The only reply he got from the Viceroy infuriated him. Besides ordering him to stop capturing and selling slaves, it forbade him to leave Mexico without permission.

In Monclova, where he made his home, Castaño called the townspeople and farmers together, told them what he had learned about a fabulously bountiful land in the north, and proposed that they join in an expedition that would make them all wealthy. To convince them that he was telling the truth, he produced assays of extraordinarily high-grade silver which he said had come from mines up the Río Grande. Castaño's talents as a salesman, bolstered by the dishonest silver trick, won over the settlers, and they agreed to go.

The Castaño Expedition left Monclova late in July, 1590, in violation of royal laws and the Viceroy's orders. It is historically important because it was the first attempt to establish a permanent colony in the vast land Coronado had discovered half a century earlier, and it took the first wheeled vehicles into territory that would become the American Southwest. The expedition, however, was a tragic failure.

In the long column which crawled toward the Río Grande in the late summer of 1590 were a hundred and seventy men, women and children—virtually the entire population of Monclova—a train of supply wagons, a large herd of livestock, and two brass cannon. As the expedition moved along, horsemen were sent to capture Indians and enslave them as servants and camptenders.

Castaño might easily have followed the well-known trail down the Conchos, but, completely a victim of his dreams, he thought that by opening a new route to the north he might come upon people and treasures earlier explorers had not found. He spent approximately six weeks in finding a passage to the Río Grande, which the company crossed at some point between the present-day Texas towns of Del Rio and Eagle Pass. There they recuperated from the hard journey until October 1. Starting on, they found themselves in a country that in places was impassable. Only after more weeks of struggle were they able to reach the Pecos and find a feasible trail northward into the land that would become New Mexico.

Following the Pecos River, the route over which Espejo had returned, they reached the great Pecos Pueblo on the last day of the year 1590. The inhabitants rejected Castaño's overtures of friendship and his requests for food. A fight followed, several Indians were killed, and under the fire of Spanish guns the others fled. Castaño's men raided the town and took the provisions so badly needed by the company.

Undeterred by cold and snow, Castaño explored the country, visited numerous pueblos, most of which willingly complied with his demands, and traveled westward through Glorieta Pass. He passed near the site of Santa Fe, and continued on to the Río Grande. Throughout

January and February, 1591, small contingents of the expedition searched for mines. The valley of the Río Grande in northern New Mexico, as all previous explorers had learned, was well populated. Castaño stopped at a score or more of towns in which the people lived well and were amply supplied with food.

Early in March, Castaño selected the pueblo of Santo Domingo as his headquarters, his "capital." He contemplated sending a party back to Mexico to inform the Viceroy of his "great achievement," and to request reinforcements. He had accomplished what no other conquistador had been able to do . . . he had conquered New Mexico, brought men, women and children to a bountiful land, established a colony in which he would develop fine farms. Prosperity was sure to follow. Rich ores certainly would be discovered.

Suddenly Castaño's dream was shattered.

He was riding in the country on a spring day when messengers from Santo Domingo overtook him with the news that a company of Spaniards, commanded by Captain Juan Morlete, had arrived from Mexico. Castaño's first thought was that they had been sent by the Viceroy Velasco to congratulate him and to make arrangements to strengthen the colony. Morlete in days past had been a political rival, but undoubtedly, in view of his great victory in subduing New Mexico for the King, the enmity that had once existed between them would be forgotten. Now Morlete would be his good friend and aide in the development of New Mexico. He hurried back to meet him.

As Castaño rode into the plaza of Santo Domingo he found forty Spanish soldiers encamped there. Morlete came forward, and the two men embraced and exchanged warm greetings. Stating that he had come with royal orders, Morlete took some papers from his pocket and read aloud from them:

"When by God's favor you reach Gaspar Castaño and his people, you will use every mild and prudent means you can to persuade them to give up their expedition and return with you, since that would be the best course for them . . . you will bring them back in reasonable comfort; but you must always remember that you are conducting them as prisoners . . . and you will take away their weapons."

All slaves held by Castaño were to be returned to their homes, and "you will show all possible friendliness and good treatment to the Indians, explaining to them . . . that from now on they may be able to live in complete security." When Castaño and his colonists had been arrested, Morlete was to impound all their goods, "and after drawing up an inventory, you will bring everything to Mexico City, including all their wagons." The signature on the documents, which bore official seals, was that of the Viceroy, Don Luis de Velasco.

Castaño took the papers from Morlete's hand, placed them on his head, and then kissed them. He would submit to the commands "of his king and lord" without resistance. Morlete, knowing well Castaño's courage and violent nature, as well as his record as a lawbreaker, took no chances. He had Castaño shackled and placed under guard.

On an April day, when the New Mexico country was beautiful with the full flowering of spring, the weary and discouraged colonists, the trail-worn livestock, and the creaking wagons, all guarded by Morlete's soldiers, started down the long Río Grande road to Mexico.

Castaño was never released from the shackles. During the days on which the column rested he busied himself in writing a long letter to the Viceroy in which he proclaimed his innocence of any wrongdoing and appealed for mercy. In compliance with the law, he reminded the Viceroy, he had sent an emissary to Mexico City to inform the government of his plans to undertake the colonization of New Mexico.

He did not deny in his letter that he had received a reply telling him that the Viceroy had rejected his proposal. He had then sent another military officer to Mexico City to explain the project in detail. Confident that it would be approved, he had organized his company and had started, "because circumstances forced me to depart in order to hold my people, who were beginning to leave me. . . ." He had purposely traveled slowly and had waited several weeks on the Río Grande so that a messenger from the Viceroy might overtake him. At last he could wait no longer, and he had crossed the Río Grande and had "pressed forward with my entire company, despite many hardships, seeking and finding a wagon route, whereby in my judgment I rendered a very considerable service to his Majesty. . . ."

His discoveries, Castaño told the Viceroy, "will greatly facilitate the execution of your Grace's plan for settlement of the land, as his Majesty has urged you to do. . . . The many things I saw in the said land indicate that this route will prove most effective in encouraging many people to go there; for I have traveled over it with wagons, and all that was reported or seen in the past is negligible in comparison with what has now been brought to light."

Castaño threw himself upon the mercy of the Viceroy, asking for an early trial, and stating that he was "sadly exhausted and broken in health. . . . People will find that I am as obedient and humble now as I have always been and shall continue to be, not at all like the person pictured in the accusations heaped against me."

In March, 1593, Gaspar Castaño was sentenced by the Audencia [Judicial Court] of Mexico to serve six years in exile in the Philippines. He was killed there in a revolt of Chinese galley slaves.

Castaño never knew that the Council of the Indies in Spain, to which his case had been appealed, had revoked the sentence imposed on him by the Audencia of Mexico, and had ruled that he was innocent.

11 / A GREAT NEW PROVINCE

In 1593 a small force of cavalry, commanded by Captain Francisco Leyva de Bonilla, was patrolling the barren country along the Conchos River in northern Mexico. They had been sent out by the governor of Nueva Viscaya to capture and punish renegade Indians who had been raiding cattle herds.

Captain Bonilla had other thoughts in mind. He had schemed with an adventurer named Antonio Gutiérrez de Humana to go to New Mexico in search of the silver mines reported to exist there. When Humana joined him with servants and recruits from Santa Bárbara, they set out. A few of the soldiers who had not known of the plot before starting refused to take part in it and turned back. But most of the men were willing to join in the adventure, even though they were aware of the sad experiences of Castaño and his colony.

In violation of royal decrees, the Bonilla-Humana Expedition pushed down the Conchos to the Río

Grande and turned north. After weeks of hard travel they reached the pueblos on the river above the present community of Bernalillo, New Mexico, and established their headquarters at San Ildefonso.

From Indians in this area they heard about a "fabulously rich province" called Quivira which lay far to the northeast. It was the same old tale with which Turk had lured Coronado on his fruitless journey to the buffalo plains. Bonilla and Humana swallowed it, and left with dreams no less exciting than those which had been held by Coronado, Chamuscado, Espejo and Castaño. Only one person would live to tell what happened.

Exactly where the Bonilla-Humana company wandered during the summer of 1593 is not a matter of historical record, but it is known that they passed the great Pecos Pueblo, and "traveling slowly and resting occasionally, they reached the buffalo in a month."

Going on toward the northeast, "the farther inland they went, the larger was the number of buffalo they saw. After traveling for fifteen days more by short marches, they reached two large rivers, and beyond them many rancherias [Indian villages] with a large number of inhabitants. Farther on, in a plain, they came to a very large settlement . . . one of the two rivers they crossed earlier flowed through this pueblo . . . in some places between the houses there were fields of corn, calabashes, and beans. The natives were very numerous but received the Spaniards peacefully and furnished them with abundant supplies of food."

Although archeologists and Spanish scholars have

been unable to establish the exact route taken to the "two large rivers," they agree that the Bonilla-Humana Expedition reached the country that would become American Kansas. In a camp, somewhere on the vast Kansas plains, Bonilla and Humana had a bitter argument. The cause of the discord is not known, but they may have disagreed over the route to be taken. After the quarrel Humana sulked in his tent. At last he sent a soldier to summon Bonilla, "who came, dressed in shirt and breeches. Before he reached the tent Humana went out to meet him, drew a knife from his pocket, unsheathed it, and stabbed Captain Bonilla twice, from which he soon afterward died. He was buried at once."

Frightened by the tragic turn of affairs, five Indian servants deserted. Four of them died while attempting to make their way back to Mexico. The survivor, known only as Jusepe, fell into the hands of a band of Apaches. After being held captive for a year, he escaped and found safety in a pueblo on the upper Río Grande. Several years later the story of his experiences was recorded by Spaniards.

But Jusepe's account was not the entire story of the Bonilla-Humana Expedition. After murdering his partner, Humana continued the search for the legendary treasures of Quivira, but just where the company went is not known.

One unconfirmed story said they went farther north and east. Another report, equally without proof of its accuracy, said they went west and reached a small stream in what is now southeastern Colorado. One night when

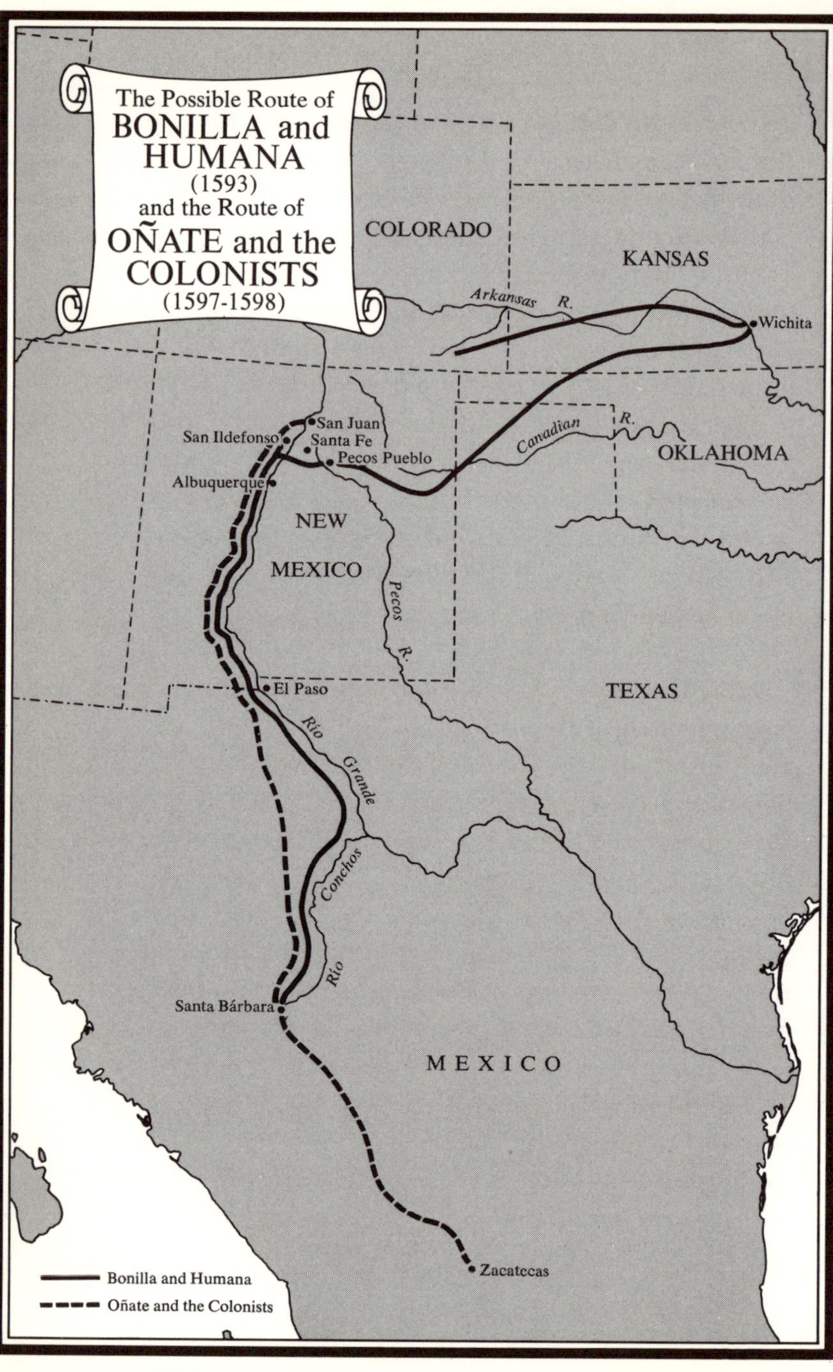

The Possible Route of
BONILLA and HUMANA
(1593)
and the Route of
OÑATE and the
COLONISTS
(1597-1598)
COLORADO
KANSAS
Arkansas R.
Wichita
San Juan
San Ildefonso
Santa Fe
Albuquerque
Pecos Pueblo
Canadian R.
OKLAHOMA
NEW
MEXICO
Pecos R.
TEXAS
El Paso
Rio Grande
Conchos
Río
Santa Bárbara
MEXICO
Zacatecas
Bonilla and Humana
Oñate and the Colonists

they were camped in a pleasant place along this stream, Indians, thought to be Comanches, set fire to the surrounding grass, and killed every man of the expedition as they attempted to escape through the smoke.

Years later—so the tale goes—a party of explorers found a number of rusted Spanish guns and swords in a grove of cottonwoods along the small stream. They gave it the name *El Río de Las Ánimas Perdidas en Purgatorio* —The River of Lost Souls in Purgatory—for they believed that the rusted arms had belonged to Humana and his men.

One fact alone remains indisputable: the Indian servant, Jusepe, was the only survivor of the Bonilla-Humana Expedition.

More than a decade had passed since the Spanish King had suggested, if not ordered, that a contract be negotiated with some responsible man for the founding of a permanent colony in New Mexico. The Sovereign's instructions in the matter had been rigid: the man selected must have demonstrated his capacity for leadership; he must be a competent administrator; he must solemnly pledge to uphold all laws governing colonization and the treatment of Indians, under pain of severe punishment; his religious faith and his piety must be beyond question; and, preferably, he must be wealthy in his own right.

Two Viceroys and many high church and government officials of New Spain had given a great deal of thought to the problem, but it had not been resolved. To begin with, a man who could fulfill all the qualifications demanded by the King was difficult to find. Numerous persons had been considered, but in each case stumbling blocks had been encountered.

The chief obstacle was money. The man who agreed to undertake the great project would be required to bear a large part of the expense. The theory was that with his own fortune invested in the expedition he would scrupulously uphold the trust placed in him and would spare no effort to make it a success. If such an arrangement was based on logic, however, it also created serious difficulties. Several acceptable candidates had been unwilling to endanger their own financial security to the extent required. Some simply didn't have the necessary funds. The honors of being chosen to lead the conquest and of being the first governor of the new province were certainly to be coveted. But what other rewards would be guaranteed? If a man sold his property and pledged his other wealth, what assurance would he have that he would benefit for his sacrifices, or even get his investment back?

Just before he left office in 1590, the Viceroy Villamanrique had recommended that a contract be signed with a wealthy mine owner, Juan Bautista de Lomas. He had requested that his successor, Velasco, complete the agreement. Velasco considered the terms of the proposal extravagant, and had rejected it. It was his opinion that Villamanrique had promised too many rewards and had granted too much authority to Lomas.

Material profit, Velasco wrote the King in 1592, should not be the main consideration. He thought it preferable for his Majesty "to grant such favors as you may choose to the persons who have served and aided you well [in colonizing New Mexico] after the gains are achieved . . . rather than you should make the grants now, without knowing what is being given away. . . . Thus, I have decided to suspend the expedition until your Majesty has ordered an investigation of the matter. . . ." Velasco expressed the belief that the delay would be "less objectionable . . . than an attempt to avoid expense by extending your hand to someone who perchance stretches out his own for purposes of self-interest but withdraws it when the purpose is the service of God and your Majesty." Lomas didn't get the contract.

More than a year later Velasco was still struggling with the problem. By exiling Castaño to the Philippines, he wrote the King, "we prevented the growth of obstacles to the exploration and pacification of New Mexico which might have resulted. . . ."

He could assure his Majesty, however that he was "engaged in preparations and negotiations designed to facilitate the undertaking in New Mexico and to lessen the drain upon the royal treasury. Nevertheless, to avoid a contract with such outrageous conditions as those asked by Lomas, some expense may be unavoidable, such as the cost of the friars who will take part in the expedition, since your Majesty invariably provides whatever is needed for them in such explorations. I am making arrangements for the speedy execution of this project with the least possible expense to the royal treasury, and I shall keep your Majesty informed of developments."

In 1595 Viceroy Velasco found the man he wanted.

He was Don Juan de Oñate of Zacatecas, a member of one of the wealthiest and most prominent families in Mexico.

Oñate owned great ranches, mines and other property, some of which he had inherited, but much of which he had acquired through his own efforts. His father, Don Cristobal, had been a noted conquistador and Governor of Nueva Galicia. His wife, Doña Isabel, was a granddaughter of the famed Hernando Cortez, conqueror of Mexico, and a great-granddaughter of the Aztec Emperor Montezuma.

Velasco had been right when he had predicted to the King that "no one will care to enter into a contract for this venture without assurances of great advantages and profit," or without being awarded large ranches and being paid tribute by the Pueblo Indians. The contract he finally gave Oñate made him Governor and Captain-General of the Province of New Mexico. He would hold title to "30 leagues of land with all the vassals [Indians] thereon." He would receive an annual salary of eight thousand gold ducats, considered enormous at the time. He would not have to pay a "royal tax" on any mines he discovered and operated. He and his officers could hold in bondage large numbers of Indian laborers. He would have the right to exact tribute to support the colony from all natives in his realm. Eleven Franciscan friars would go with him "for the spiritual well-being of all," and the government would pay their expenses and would furnish them "with fitting church accoutrements." Besides supplying Oñate with adequate quantities of arms and ammunition, the royal treasury would give him $4,000 and lend him $6,000 to help defray the cost of launching the expedition.

In return for all these honors and privileges, Oñate agreed to recruit a force of several hundred soldiers and colonists at his own expense. He also guaranteed to see that they were supplied with the necessary transportation and foodstuffs, as well as herds of cattle and other animals to start a livestock industry in New Mexico.

After five years of wrestling with the problem, Velasco had been obliged to agree to terms no less extravagant and costly than those demanded by other men which he had rejected. He was leaving office, however, and he wanted to please the King by making the best arrangements he could for the colonization of New Mexico before departing.

The contract with Oñate brought a storm of protest from jealous rivals who had hoped to win the great prize. Velasco's successor as Viceroy, the Count of Monterey, found himself faced with an unpleasant situation. Although he had assured Velasco that he would uphold the agreement with Oñate, he soon found reasons for delaying the expedition. Almost everyone of prominence, it seemed, had something uncomplimentary to say about Oñate, and ugly rumors about his unfitness and dishonesty were being widely circulated. Oñate was accused of being a squanderer, of failing to pay his just debts. He was charged with having recruited an army of thugs and wastrels, with borrowing money under false pretenses, with deceiving the King and Velasco by making claims which were without foundation. He was neither a good administrator nor a capable leader. Soldiers would not obey him. If he got to New Mexico he would defraud the government and set himself up as a dictator.

Monterey disliked most the terms in the contract which granted Oñate supreme judicial powers—the right of life and death—in the new colony, and made him independent of the Mexican Government in deciding problems relating to war and finances. He insisted that these provisions be revised so that Oñate's authority in such matters was more restricted. Also, he ordered that an inventory be made of all equipment, arms and supplies that Oñate would take with him.

Now it was revealed that Monterey was in favor of cancelling Oñate's contract and giving a new one to a friend, Pedro Ponce de León. The Viceroy had written the King proposing that the expedition be delayed "until further investigations could be made," and the King had agreed.

Oñate was not without influential friends, however, and they rallied to his support. Although angered and disappointed, he went doggedly ahead with his plans. The inspection and inventory Monterey had ordered were made in July, 1596, and Oñate moved a part of his force north to Santa Bárbara. He expected to receive any day orders from Monterey to proceed.

In September a letter came from Monterey notifying Oñate of the King's agreement to the delay the Viceroy had requested. Oñate was commanded not to go any farther. If he disobeyed, severe penalties would be inflicted on him, and his contract would be cancelled.

Oñate obeyed and attempted to conceal the bad news from his colonists, but it leaked out. A number of men with families, some soldiers, and several priests, went back to their homes. Oñate firmly refused to give up. He had spent immense sums of his own money for equipment, livestock and supplies, and he did not propose to abandon the enterprise. Most of the colonists remained loyal, and his friends brought new pressure to bear on Monterey to allow the force to proceed.

More inspections and inventories were ordered. The months passed. More soldiers and civilians deserted. To the strenuous protests of Oñate and his friends, the Viceroy replied that he was unable to act without further orders from the King. One early account of the situation stated that whereas Oñate's foes wanted to break up the expedition altogether, the Viceroy wanted to keep it intact until he could find a way of giving the command to Pedro Ponce de León.

If this were true, Monterey was disappointed. He did not get the support he had expected to receive from the King. Moreover, some powerful religious officials were charging that Oñate's long delay was the work of the Devil, who was trying to prevent the souls of thousands of Indians in New Mexico from being saved. Even a Viceroy would have to take heed of such charges.

In any case, Monterey gave up the fight, and in the fall of 1597 sent Oñate word to prepare for a final inspection. One historian of the time declared it was the Viceroy's belief that, having lost so many men and used up so many supplies in the long wait, Oñate would fail to pass the inspection. Monterey himself, however, stated that the inspectors were secretly instructed to deal leniently with Oñate, and overlook small violations of the contract.

Whatever the truth, the inspectors found "all in order," and in January, 1598, Oñate was given permission to proceed—more than three years after he had signed the agreement with Velasco.

Throughout the spring and summer of 1598 a great moving dust cloud rose above the northbound trail along the Río Grande. It was caused by eighty-three heavily loaded wagons, troops of horsemen, and a great herd of more than seven thousand head of livestock. With the long column, which stretched out for nearly four miles, were one hundred and thirty families of settlers, two hundred and seventy single men—soldiers, craftsmen, and hopeful young adventurers—eleven Franciscan friars, and scores of Indian and Negro servants, wranglers and camptenders. In the lead, surrounded by his staff—all splendidly arrayed in shining armor, plumed helmets, silk and lace shirts, and fine Cordovan boots with tasseled spurs—rode the handsome Don Juan Oñate.

He was already Governor, Captain-General and Chief Judicial Officer of the land, for he had formally and legally taken possession of it—of all its pastures, forests, mountains, valleys and rivers, of all its pueblos, and of all its native inhabitants for God, for King, and for himself.

The Indians were friendly, giving freely of their food and opening their houses to the Spaniards. On a midsummer day in Santo Domingo (on the Río Grande above Bernalillo) they found two Mexican Indians, Thomas and Christopher, who had remained when Castaño was taken away in chains with his soldiers and settlers. This was a great stroke of good luck. Although they had been at Santo Domingo for seven years, happily married to Pueblo women, they had not forgotten how to speak Spanish, and they had become fluent in several Indian languages. Oñate at once took them under his supervision as interpreters. Leaders from more than thirty surrounding towns soon came to pay their respects to the Governor. Thomas and Christopher were the links of communication between the Spaniards and the Indians. In a solemn ceremony an agreement was negotiated under which the Pueblo chiefs swore allegiance to God, the Spanish King, and to Oñate.

The column moved on up the Río Grande. Oñate made a careful inspection of the numerous pueblos along the route. On July 11, 1598, he stopped where two imposing towns stood, one on each side of the river, in a beautiful setting. Hills and mesas rolled away in the background, as if supporting the turquoise sky. Below them fields of corn and other crops ripened in the warm sun.

The two pueblos were called Yuque and Yunque. Fifty-seven years before a contingent of Coronado's army had visited them and had left a cross in the plaza of the pueblo on the east bank. The cross had long since disappeared, but in memory of the men who had erected it, Oñate gave the place the name of San Juan de los Caballeros.

With proper formalities, he announced that the Prov-

At the pueblos of Yuque and Yunque, Oñate and his group of colonists officially founded the Province of New Mexico.

ince of New Mexico—reaching from the buffalo plains of Quivira to the deserts of the Colorado River bordering California, and only God knew how far to the north —had been founded, and San Juan would be its capital.